BLOOD ON THEIR HANDS

BLOOD ON THEIR HANDS

GENERAL JOHAN BOOYSEN REVEALS HIS TRUTH

Jessica Pitchford

PAN MACMILLAN SOUTH
AFRICA

First published in 2016
by Pan Macmillan South Africa
Private Bag X19
Northlands
Johannesburg
2116

www.panmacmillan.co.za

ISBN 978-1-77010-477-8
e-ISBN 978-1-77010-478-5

© 2016 Jessica Pitchford

All rights reserved. No part of this publication may be reproduced, stored in or introduced into a retrieval system, or transmitted, in any form or by any means (electronic, mechanical, photocopying, recording or otherwise), without the prior written permission of the publisher. Any person who does any unauthorised act in relation to this publication may be liable to criminal prosecution and civil claims for damages.

The views and opinions expressed in the text that follows do not necessarily reflect those of the publisher.

Editing by Tanya Pampalone
Proofreading by Sean Fraser
Design and typesetting by Fire and Lion
Cover design by publicide
Cover photographs by Ian Carbutt/ *The Witness* and Gerhard de Bruin
Printed and bound by Shumani Mills Communications, Parow, Cape Town
SW62276

The meetings, interactions and events described in this book are in the public domain in one form or another – via sources ranging from affidavits, forensic reports, court submissions and official inquiries to media coverage and opinion pieces. In some cases, parties have been offered right of reply in terms of the issues raised in these pages. The responses have been incorporated where appropriate.

Every effort has been made to ensure the factual accuracy of the contents of this book, but should any errors have occurred, the publisher and author apologise and would welcome any information that would enable them to amend any mistakes in future editions.

This book is dedicated to those in the criminal justice system who are honest and true to their profession, and to my grandchildren, Lané, Mieke, Malan and Mila, and any others to come. – JB

CONTENTS

	Cast of Characters	xi
1	21 March 1960	1
2	Billy the Kid	13
3	Cops and Robbers	18
4	Shobashobane	28
5	Highway Heists	35
6	Cato Manor	44
7	The Assassination of Lieutenant Colonel Chonco	53
8	Cele, Mdluli and the Ground Coverage Report	69
9	Provincial Commissioner Lieutenant General Ngobeni and the Connected Businessman	75
10	'(2)' in the Boot	86
11	The Fifth Column	94
12	The Plot Thickens	106
13	The Racketeers	116
14	Arrested	123
15	The Witnesses who Weren't	129
16	The Evidence that Wasn't	143
17	Booysen vs Jiba	152
18	Rollmops and Corruption Busters	168
19	Suspended Again	175
20	Round Seven	182
21	Blood on their Hands	192
	Postscript	205
	Notes	207
	Acknowledgements	208

CAST OF CHARACTERS

THE COPS
Johan Booysen – Major General in the South African Police Services; KZN provincial head of Directorate for Priority Crime Investigation (Hawks)
Pat Brown – Major General; KZN provincial head of detectives. Retired
Bongani Ntanjana – KZN deputy provincial police commissioner. Deceased
Deena Moodley – Major General; former KZN provincial head of Crime Intelligence
Lawrence Kemp – Brigadier; SAPS KZN Provincial Finance head
Zethembe Chonco – Lieutenant Colonel; SAPS taxi violence coordinator whose assassination in 2008 inadvertently led to the suspension of Booysen and Cato Manor
Eddie van Rensburg – Lieutenant Colonel, investigating officer KZN 26 case
Willie Olivier – Lieutenant Colonel; former commander of Cato Manor. Retired
Mossie Mostert – Warrant Officer; Cato Manor. Retired
RC Maharaj – Warrant Officer; Cato Manor; killed on duty in 2011
Inkosi Mbongeleni Zondi – Zulu chief and former policeman; killed in 2009

THE TAXI UNDERWORLD
Bongani Mkhize – KwaMaphumulo Taxi Association boss who allegedly conspired to kill Lieutenant Colonel Chonco and Inkosi Zondi; shot dead by police

Swayo Mkhize – Taxi industry assassin and nephew of taxi boss Bongani Mkhize. Deceased

Li Buthelezi – Taxi owner who allegedly conspired to kill Chonco; shot dead by Cato Manor

Moses Dlamini – KwaMaphumulo Taxi Association security guard

Magojela Ndimande – Taxi owner who allegedly conspired to kill Chonco; shot dead by Cato Manor

Badumile Ndimande – Brother of Magojela; shot dead by Cato Manor

Sifiso Ndimande – Nephew of Magojela; shot dead by Cato Manor

THE SO-CALLED INFORMERS

Rajen Aiyer – Colonel and commander of Durban Organised Crime, of which Cato Manor was a sub-section; 2006–2009

Aris Danikas – Police reservist 2001–2008; *Sunday Times*/state 'source' against Booysen and Cato Manor

Simphiwe Mathonsi – Hearsay state witness. Deceased

Bheki Mthiyane, aka Ndlondlo – Police informer and hearsay witness against Booysen and Cato Manor. Deceased

Zanele Zondi – Taxi association member and alleged informer for Booysen and Cato Manor

THE PANDAY CASE

Thoshan Panday – Durban multimillionaire businessman and SAPS contractor

Deebo Mzobe – Thoshan Panday business associate; Zuma cousin

Edward Zuma – Son of President Jacob Zuma

Navin Madhoe – Colonel; SAPS section head Acquisition Management KZN Supply Chain Management and Thoshan Panday co-accused

Aswin Narainpershad – Captain; SAPS Supply Chain Management and Thoshan Panday co-accused

Kevin Stephen – Captain; SAPS member whom Panday allegedly tried to bribe

Deena Govender – Hawks warrant officer; arranged meeting between Madhoe and Booysen to discuss dropping investigation against Panday

Sandesh Dhaniram – Navin Madhoe associate and Booysen informant

Brian Padayachee – Colonel in KZN Crime Intelligence; Booysen informant

THE TOP BRASS
Hamilton Ngidi – KZN provincial police commissioner, 1999–2009
Mmamonnye Ngobeni – KZN provincial police commissioner; appointed 2009, suspended 2016
Bheki Cele – Former national police commissioner; 2009–2011
Nhlanhla Mkhwanazi – Acting national police commissioner, 2011–2012
Riah Phiyega – National police commissioner, 2012–2015 suspended
Nobulele Mbekela – Deputy national commissioner, suspended 2015
Anwa Dramat – National head of Directorate for Priority Crime Investigation (Hawks), 2009–2015 (suspended 2014, resigned 2015)
Berning Ntlemeza – National head of Directorate for Priority Crime Investigation (Hawks), 2015–present
Richard Mdluli – Suspended Crime Intelligence chief appointed 2009, suspended 2011, reappointed March 2012, suspended May 2012–present
Nathi Mthethwa – Safety and security minister, 2009–2014
Nathi Nhleko – Police minister, 2014–present

THE NATIONAL PROSECUTING AUTHORITY
Mxolisi Nxasana – National Director of Public Prosecutions, 2013–2015
Shaun Abrahams – National Director of Public Prosecutions, 2015–present
Nomgcobo Jiba – Deputy head of NPA who, as acting head, signed authorisation to charge Booysen, and was charged with fraud and perjury
Anthony Mosing – NPA Advocate and Jiba assistant in Cato Manor case
Lawrence Mrwebi – Advocate and former NPA Specialised Commercial Crime Unit head; special director of Public Prosecutions, 2011–present
Bheki Manyathi – Senior state advocate Durban Directorate of Public Prosecutions, 2005–2013; recommended that Madhoe and Panday be indicted
Simphiwe Mlotshwa – Advocate and former acting KZN Prosecutions head; replaced in 2012 after refusing to charge Booysen without evidence and refusing to withdraw charges in Amigos corruption case
Moipone Noko – Replaced Simphiwe Mlotshwa as KZN Prosecutions boss in 2012, dropped charges against Madhoe and Panday; recommended reinstatement of charges against Booysen
Sello Maema – Cato Manor prosecutor in racketeering case
Raymond Mathenjwa – Cato Manor prosecutor in racketeering case

THE INVESTIGATORS

Vasan Subramoney – Colonel, KZN Hawks investigator, 2010–2011
Hans van Loggerenberg – Colonel, KZN Hawks investigator. Retired
Len Sheriff – Colonel, KZN Hawks investigator
Kobus Roelofse – Hawks Colonel who investigated abuse of police secret fund controlled by Richard Mdluli
Simon Madonsela – Brigadier; Booysen associate and Organised Crime officer who investigated abuse of police secret fund in KZN
Jan Mabula – Hawks Major General investigating Booysen and Cato Manor
Zodwa Mokoena – Brigadier investigating Booysen and Cato Manor
Tsietso Mano – Colonel investigating Booysen and Cato Manor. Deceased
Pharasa Ncube – Colonel investigating Booysen and Cato Manor
Alfred Khana – Hawks Major General investigating Booysen and Olivier for fraud

ON THE SIDELINES

Carl van der Merwe – Booysen and Cato Manor criminal lawyer
Nazeer Cassim SC – Advocate and chairman of SAPS disciplinary into Booysen
Thereza Botha – investigator who did cellphone analysis in KZN 26 and Chonco cases
Moses Dlamini – Spokesman for Independent Police Investigative Directorate, suspended 2016
Robert McBride – Independent Police Investigative Directorate head; appointed 2014, suspended 2015
Shadrack Sibiya – Gauteng Hawks head, 2010–2015; dismissed for alleged illegal rendition of Zimbabwean criminal suspects
Jabulani Zikhali – Major General, replaced Booysen as head of KZN Hawks in 2016

- 1 -
21 MARCH 1960

Three Air Force Harvard trainers roared overhead, seconds apart, the tips of their propellers breaking the sound barrier. Standing in the garden, Johan was both terrified and transfixed. The noise was like nothing he'd heard before. He rushed inside shouting for his mother.

Makkie Booysen told him there were problems outside town – in Sharpeville. 'Town' was Vanderbijlpark, modelled around one of the world's most up-to-date steel works and the prize project of inventor and engineer, Dr HJ van der Bijl, who'd been in charge of the post-World War economy in South Africa. The Vaal Triangle towns of Vanderbijl, Vereeniging and Sasolburg were economically vital and fitted a broader vision: loyal parastatal employees whose residence would be tied to their employment. Whites-only neighbourhoods reflected the cost and status that went with where you worked. Blacks lived in the surrounding townships of Bophelong, Sharpeville and Sebokeng and provided cheap labour.[1]

The Booysen home was modest. But there was electricity, an indoor bathroom and running water in the kitchen. It never occurred to Johan that they were poor.

I was the firstborn and there were seven kids after me. So maybe I got everything new – instead of the hand-me-downs. I do remember that we all shared a toothbrush. It didn't seem a big deal. Our car was so old we had to start it with two wires. My brothers and I used to steal milk from the van that did the deliveries. We'd drink it straight from the bottle until we were so full we couldn't move.

The Harvards he'd seen flying overhead, he learned in later years, had been sent to intimidate the residents of Sharpeville, 10 kilometres away, where 69 people had been shot dead while protesting outside the police station.

The following day, Prime Minister HF Verwoerd told parliament that the anti-pass protests at Sharpeville weren't against the government. Johan says his parents would've completely believed this.

I came from a conservative Afrikaans family. We believed what we were taught, what we read in the newspapers, heard on the radio. It was my dream to be a policeman and three of my four brothers became policemen. That smart blue uniform with gold buttons looked impressive. It was nothing like the current-day operational uniform. My mother joined a shooting club when I was at school and I went with her. I was a natural.

He was also a natural at sports: quick on the athletics track, tactical on the rugby field.

My mother was extremely proud of me. I was her blue-eyed boy. She and my dad wouldn't miss a sporting event at school. By the time I reached the finish, or the try line, my dad would be hitting the ground and yelling. In relays, I would be standing waiting for the baton and he would be shouting 'Hier kom hy nou!' ['Here he comes now!'] Then he would dart across the field to the finish line. Sometimes he'd run with us.

Dad, Phill, was a boilermaker, cutting steel to build big tanks and pipes at any one of the surrounding industrial sites attached to Iscor or Sasol. He was also a wanderer: he got bored easily, changed jobs often, moved house frequently.

When Johan was 11, they went on holiday to visit a friend of his parents who'd moved from the Vaal to the Natal South Coast.

A month later they packed up and left the 'Vuil Driehoek' ('Foul Triangle') for the fresh air of Warner Beach on the South Coast.

We travelled there in an Escort panel van – six kids crammed in the back with no windows and my grandmother smoking all the way. To this day I hate cigarette smoke.

Johan was thrust into an English environment.

There were no Afrikaans schools in Warner Beach. I couldn't even have a basic conversation in English, but found myself at an English school. Luckily I could run. On my first day there we had to do an athletics heat. I won. Then I felt accepted.

When an Afrikaans school opened in Amanzimtoti, 3 kilometres from Warner Beach, Johan moved over. But he still wasn't the slightest bit interested in the academic side of school.

If there was homework that I hadn't done, which was almost always, I would arrive at school early and persuade the brighter kids to allow me to copy theirs. Come exams I hadn't a clue what was going on.

After failing Standard 9, Johan decided he'd had enough of school. His father had left in Standard 6, his mother in Standard 7, so they had no problem with their eldest son pursuing his dream.

It was 1974. In white South Africa, the Rosenkowitz sextuplets were born; BJ Vorster called an early election alarmed at decolonisation moves in Mozambique and Angola; the British Lions began a controversial 22-match tour of South Africa and Rhodesia; and Anneline Kriel was crowned Miss World. In black South Africa, activists Onkgopotse Tiro and Adolphus Mvemve were killed by parcel bombs in Botswana and Zambia; Winnie Mandela was sentenced to six months in prison for meeting with another banned person; and Chris Hani travelled to Lesotho to set up an ANC base.

Sixteen-year-old Johan enlisted with the police. There were two intakes a year and he joined in February. He enrolled in Durban and the recruits were put on a train to police college in Pretoria.

There were 36 of us in a dormitory and we had communal showers, with inspection at the crack of dawn. We were allowed no contact with home for the first month except for occasional calls, and there was usually a fight to use the pay phones.

Phill and Makkie came to visit him after the first month and realised their son wasn't coping, so suggested he pack it in. He bought his discharge, went back home and joined the railways. In those days it was a place that provided sheltered employment for Afrikaners. Johan got a job as a clerk, filling in waybills at Merebank, a station in an industrial part of Durban. It was mind-numbingly boring and he lasted six months.

School, I realised, hadn't been so bad after all. One of my old teachers, Mr van Wyk, also encouraged me to go back and finish; he thought I had potential. For the first time, I did well and I realised I actually could sit down and study. I joined the school cadets and was an ace, having perfected marching during my month at police college.

He'd completed Standard 9 and was in matric when his girlfriend, Letithia, fell pregnant and Johan found himself with no means to support an impending family. He enrolled to join the police again and got married in July 1976. The next intake was only the following year, so he worked as a student constable at the Amanzimtoti Police Station, lived with his in-laws and studied for his matric through correspondence.

Willie Olivier, who was to become Johan's first sergeant, was there at the same time: 'I took one look at this oke – thin as a beanpole – and thought he won't make it. No ways.'

But Johan did, spending his days as the office dogsbody, sorting and helping to deliver summonses and warrants of arrest.

We had our baby in September 76; I got my matric and the following year I went back to police college. Letithia and my son came along and stayed with a couple my parents knew in Danville and I would go there every weekend. So at least I got a break from college, which was a very disciplined environment.

In 1977, after graduating, he went back to Amanzimtoti as a constable with the uniformed branch. By this time Olivier was the charge office sergeant. Morning parade with him was designed to wake you up, remembers Johan.

We'd stand to attention, he'd check to see that our brass buckles and buttons and stars were shiny. If he noticed our hair over our collars, we'd have to go for a haircut after parade and make up the time after hours. Then he'd make us do an about turn, draw our firearms, load them and put them back in our holsters. He'd check to see if any of us had injuries in case we tried to claim for being injured on duty.

At first Johan was a patrol van driver. He'd be sent out to petty complaints – noise, vandalism, urinating in public, fights at the local pub and the theft of laundry.

It was an era when police action of any kind made the news.

21 MARCH 1960

SOUTH COAST SUN
1981

A suitcase full of stolen clothes was recovered after a chase on the freeway on Toti on Tuesday. At 1pm Officer JW Booysen of the Toti Police approached a man who was walking on the freeway carrying a suitcase. The man ran off and Officer Booysen gave chase across the freeway. An unknown Indian motorist forced the fleeing man off the road and he was apprehended. The suitcase contained clothing as well as a radio stolen during a house breaking in Doonside.

There were more serious issues too. One night an American tourist got lost and stopped in Warner Beach to ask for directions to Durban. Two men by the side of the road offered to show her the way, but instead took her along the back roads to Amanzimtoti where they raped and stabbed her to death before setting her car alight. Olivier mentioned to Johan that he knew the name of one of the suspects, a man called Njokwa, who'd sold items belonging to the murdered woman. Johan recognised the name as someone who did odd jobs for his father on a Saturday. He knew where he lived and Njokwa was brought in for questioning, positively linked to the murder, charged and got the death sentence.

Olivier and Johan became friends – they lived near each other, played rugby for the police, coached wrestling and became detectives together. Peter Bishop, who arrived at Toti as a student constable fresh from police college, remembers them as a formidable pair who weren't scared of much:

> Johan had red hair and a temperament to match. Once he was called out to the Beach Hotel to sort out a brawl. As he walked in this burly bouncer type grabbed the front of his tunic and tore it. Johan took him to the charge office, challenged him to a fistfight and won. Then they shook hands and that was that.

Johan remembers Letithia being unimpressed with the state of his uniform when he got home, covered in blood.
The other guy's blood ...

He and Olivier were also the station clowns. Their favourite trick was to put indelible fingerprint ink on door handles, telephone receivers or under desks. They delighted in seeing ears covered in black ink after answering the phone or thick smears of it on a colonel's white safari suit.

The station commander offered a reward – a day off – for whoever caught the culprits. It made Johan even more daring.

One day I went into his office with a big blob of fingerprint ink on my thumb and surreptitiously smeared it on his door handle while I stood talking to him. Five minutes after I left you should've heard the swearing. I think they suspected it was Willie and me, but were never able to prove it.

They were also extremely efficient policemen. At the end of 1982, Lieutenant Bushie Engelbrecht took over the Amanzimtoti detective branch. He mentions it in his book *A Christmas to Remember*: 'One of the first things I did ... was to replace some of the detectives with more dynamic policemen ... among them were Johan Booysen and Willie Olivier.'

Johan recalls how they would curse Bushie, who was pedantic about small details.

He'd go through a docket like a schoolteacher and cover our investigation diaries with red ink. Where's this, where's that? I had a case where the diamond in a ring had been replaced by a zirconia. The complainant only discovered this when the ring went to be valued. There was no way of knowing who'd swapped it or when. It could've been a family member, a staff member, the jeweller or the valuator. I wanted to get on with other investigations, but Bushie refused to let me close the case until I had interviewed a dozen jewellers. It taught me to look at cases from all angles and give attention to detail and it stood me in good stead when I managed investigations later in my career. I became like Bushie. Today there's an absence of mentors at branch level.

Detectives wore plain clothes and Johan was dressed in a brand-new green safari suit one day when Olivier asked him to help him find a rape suspect in Umbogintwini, northeast of Amanzimtoti. They located the man, but he fled, Johan in hot pursuit, Olivier puffing behind. The suspect leapt into a river and waded across. Johan followed. On the other side, the chase resumed and the man disappeared into thick bush. Johan, out of breath and by now clad only in his sodden trousers, fired a few rounds from his Walther PPK, standard issue to detectives at the time. The man was eventually found by the dog squad and was admitted to hospital with bullet wounds to his left shoulder and hand, right leg and hip.

Johan bought another safari suit.

His first murder investigation was into the killing of a bus passenger in KwaMakhutha, a township close to Toti. Specialised units like Murder and Robbery investigated white murders, local detectives like Johan handled black murder cases. He hooked up with a Zulu detective to translate for him, bought himself a camera and a flexible ruler to take measurements – and solved the case.

Nowadays detectives would get fingerprint experts and crime scene technicians to do the photographs and drawings. Those days there was none of that. Detectives were meant to do their own free-hand drawings. I was hopeless at drawing, hence the camera and ruler.

•

So-called faction fighting was rife in the 80s, particularly in the Umbumbulu area, southwest of Durban, which became a hotbed of political violence. After three policemen were killed, Olivier, who had a good informer network, got a tip-off about the whereabouts of the weapons taken from the dead men. He and Johan went to investigate. Johan felt edgy.

Although worlds apart, it was a similar situation to Afghanistan – tricky terrain and difficult to negotiate. There was thick bush, it was hilly and the fighting clans knew it well. The most effective way of policing was to fly over the area with a chopper, check out where the izimpi *were gathering for an attack, land the chopper, seize their weapons and arrest them. We were going in by car, then on foot.*

The three policemen had been shot the weekend before while approaching warring groups. A constable who had been there testified at the inquest: 'A group of about 500 men jumped up from the bushes and all sang a war song. They started shooting at us. I threw myself down and opened fire. I saw that some of our members were retreating … I took cover and hid myself in the forest until the fighting stopped.'[2]

The Truth and Reconciliation Commission found that violence in Umbumbulu, while ascribed to tribalism, was political in nature, involving factions aligned to the ANC and to Inkatha, backed by the state:

> The conflict was often referred to as 'tribal clashes' or 'faction fighting' and was attributed to intense rivalry for land, water and jobs. The ethnic nature of the conflict supported the state's contention that political conflict in the province was 'black on black', and helped play down the failure of the security forces to intervene in a way that might have limited the scale of the suffering and loss.[3]

Whatever the underlying reasons, three policemen had died and any leads had to be followed up. Supported by members of Durban's Reaction Unit, Olivier, Johan and a sergeant called Ben Hadebe, who was Olivier's eyes and ears, set off after midnight so they wouldn't be spotted as they approached – or end up being the subject of an inquest. But Johan says they didn't really consider the consequences.

In hindsight the mission was a bit foolhardy. It was a dangerous area. We drove until the road gave way to bush then walked the last few kilometres.

Once they'd established from an informer where the weapons supposedly were, Hadebe knocked on the door of a rondavel they'd been directed to. No answer. So Johan decided to kick down the door.

Telling it now, it sounds very stupid. Once I'd made a hole, I stuck my hand in to open the door. Suddenly I felt this thud on my chest and rushed for cover.

They began shooting from 20 metres away, Johan with an Uzi and Olivier with an R1.

We were shooting at all angles, but missing. When we stopped I felt this wetness on my chest and said to Willie, 'Daar's iets nat hierso' ['Something is wet here']. I lifted up my shirt and there was a gaping hole. I'd either been shot or stabbed when I'd tried to open the door.

Olivier and one of the Reaction Unit members made a seat using R1s and tried carrying Johan to their vehicle with him perched on the rifles.

The pain got worse as they jolted me over the rough terrain. So they put me down and dragged me, arms draped over their shoulders. I was convinced I was dying. I was on medication and yelled at Willie that if I lost consciousness he should get someone to phone Letithia so she could speak to the paramedics.

By the time they got to their vehicle Olivier was so panicked he could hardly speak.

Peter Bishop, stationed at Umbumbulu at the time, heard his message come over on his police radio: 'They were in the bush, miles from anywhere – Johan could easily have died. Luckily there was a medic from the Reaction Unit who treated him until an ambulance met them on the Umbumbulu Road.'

Bushie Engelbrecht knocked on Johan's front door that morning to tell Letithia he wouldn't be home.

He spent a week in hospital. He'd been stabbed in the diaphragm; his lung nicked in the process. Thirty years later, he still has the scar. The next day newspapers carried a picture of him lying in a hospital bed, his chest strapped.

DAILY NEWS
11 FEBRUARY 1986

In a new attack on the police at strife-torn Umbumbulu last night, a detective was stabbed and shot at before five suspects in Sunday night's triple police slaying were detained.

SOUTH COAST SUN
13 FEBRUARY 1986

Detective Warrant Officer Johan Booysen had tried to force his way in but one of the suspects pushed an assegai through the door and W/O Booysen was stabbed. The assegai penetrated about 10 centimetres.

•

Before he became a detective, Johan often did patrol duty with another constable called Brian Denny, who later left the police to study law at the University of Natal. Years later, when Johan was called out to help control a protest in downtown Durban, he saw Denny, now a long-haired law student, marching along with a placard.

We had a good laugh. I thought 'typical student'. I know it sounds naive, but it never dawned on me in the 80s that South Africa was in trouble. The only news we were able to watch was the SABC and we'd see Pik Botha at the United Nations defending us, appearing very much in control. My parents read Die Vaderland *and so did I. Later I read* The Citizen.

When a car bomb ripped through the Why Not restaurant and Magoo's Bar on the Durban beachfront, popular haunts of the security branch and the military, Johan had nothing but disdain for the 22-year-old man from Wentworth who was arrested. Robert McBride was convicted and sentenced to death, but was released in 1992. Decades later, McBride and Johan would find themselves on the same side, fighting what they both perceived to be the injustices of a democratic South Africa.

I visited the scene of the Magoo's Bar bombing the morning after it happened, but it didn't stop me liking him as a person 30 years later and appreciating his work ethic. Despite where he came from and where I came from, we got on because with him, like with me, if something's wrong, it is wrong and if it is right, it is right. We share the same mindset about fighting corruption and we are able to relate, without bitterness, experiences from our past. I joke with him that he was lucky I wasn't the shooter when he escaped from the police cells in Bellair and only got hit in the leg.

Johan's favourite book in the 80s was *Operation Q-018* by Gerard Ludi. Ludi worked for the Security Branch and was instructed to infiltrate the South African Communist Party (SACP), which was an unknown entity in 1959. It took years, but Ludi eventually became trusted in leftist circles by people like Joe Slovo and Ruth First. He not only infiltrated the SACP, but was sent behind the Iron Curtain. He so impressed the Soviets that he went on a top-secret mission to China. His double life came to a crashing halt when the head of the Bureau of State Security, Hendrik van den Bergh, ordered him home to give vital evidence in the Fischer trial, resulting in Bram Fischer being sentenced to life imprisonment. Ludi became a marked man and a target for assassination.

The book and its detailed accounts of 'smashing terrorist cells' inspired Johan to get moving.

Envisaging a Ludi-like 'spy-spy' career ahead of him, he applied to join the Security Branch, in those days seen as an elite unit of intelligence officers. But he was turned down.

I applied four times. Each time I was rejected. The fifth time I got in. I passed my national diploma in police administration and did an intensive 13-week officer's course and emerged as a lieutenant.

The Security Branch was located in the same building as the Durban Central Police Station, but had its own entrance, with separate lifts. That was about as cloak-and-dagger as it got. Johan realised he wasn't going to be another Gerard Ludi. He hated the work, which involved compiling endless reports on possible security threats, many of which didn't seem particularly threatening at all. When he heard of a vacancy for a branch commander at Brighton Beach on the Bluff he applied.

I got myself out of the security branch into the detective branch. I liked action. I liked solving murders. I liked arresting suspects and taking them to court and proving the case. The workload wasn't like it is today, where a detective has no hope of solving all the cases lumped on him. Back then we would have about 30 cases per detective. If you got to 35 you would have an anxiety attack. These days each detective has about a hundred dockets. It's impossible to cope.

By this time Peter Bishop had moved from Umbumbulu to Murder and Robbery in Durban, regarded as a prestige unit, and occasionally called on Johan to assist him after he'd made an arrest. In terms of the Criminal Procedure Act, only a commissioned officer who was a neutral party could record confessions or take suspects to point out crime scenes. Many officers – like his friend Olivier – were reluctant to do this because it involved spending hours in court and being grilled on the witness stand.

Willie, with his vast informer network, was one of those less keen on making regular court appearances. Once, after arresting someone for the murder of a shopkeeper, he received a tip-off that the weapon used to commit the crime was hidden in the suspect's house in Umlazi. He took me with him and while searching the premises told me to check under the fridge in the kitchen. I fell for it. As soon as I found the gun there, I realised that he had known all along that it was there, but wanted to avoid giving evidence in court.

Olivier says he was merely giving a junior officer some experience: 'Earlier I had lifted the fridge in the kitchen and seen the gun there, but decided to leave it for him. He got so excited when he found it.'

Johan scoffs at Olivier's recollections. These days Johan knows as much about the law as many criminal attorneys, thanks in part to years and years of testifying in court. At the time it was a skill he thought he could master the more experience he gained.

It involved taking meticulous notes, being 100 per cent familiar with the case, sticking to the truth and making concessions if necessary. It's no good being an investigator unless you know what the law allows – my knowledge of criminal law, procedure and evidence has increased greatly over the years. I also studied law subjects when doing my degree.

His enthusiasm and flair caught the eye of the commander of the Durban Murder and Robbery Unit, Leonard Knipe.

Colonel Knipe asked me to join them at Murder and Robbery. I had to think about it. I was branch commander at Brighton Beach. Did I want to become second in charge – albeit of a more elite unit?

Reckoning it was probably a good career move, Johan accepted.

- 2 -

BILLY THE KID

The 90s dawned. Change was in the air. But the lines between politics and crime remained blurred. Conflict and civil war in KwaZulu intensified. There was a marked increase in attacks on police officers.

In 1991, the MK-trained ANC member and Umbumbulu warlord Sipho Mkhize was executed by notorious KwaZulu police constable Siphiwe Mvuyane, who was attached to the Umlazi Murder and Robbery Squad. The rogue cop had been implicated in more than 20 killings, mainly of ANC activists.

Mkhize's teenage son, Sibusiso, who'd received military training in the Transkei, vowed to avenge his father's death and began targeting police and IFP warlords. He tried on numerous occasions to take out Mvuyane, who was later shot dead by someone else:

> Legend has it that S'bu used to operate primarily from a van that he had modified by upgrading the engine and replacing the back seats with an open area from which to fire weapons. He would then travel around, often shooting at people from the back of his van before speeding off. Stories of his exploits range from full-on attacks on police stations to bombs set off at IFP funerals.[4]

Johan was doing admin at the Durban Murder and Robbery Unit when a sergeant, Craig Smith, rushed into his office. He said a Sergeant Botha had been shot while trying to apprehend suspects in a BMW on the Umbumbulu road. Botha had been taken to hospital, but the perpetrators were still at large.

The wounded sergeant's radio call had been heard by Warrant Officer Peter Knop of the Dog Unit, who raced to the area, as did an Air Force Alouette.

Johan and Craig Smith joined in the ground search. A minibus, later found to have been hijacked, passed them then stopped.

The occupants opened fire on a police vehicle driving behind us. I did a U-turn so Craig could return fire. There was a fierce gun battle – with AKs, Uzis and R5s. It was over very quickly. Three of the gunmen were killed, one was arrested and two fled down a gorge.

Several policemen pursued them, led by Knop with his dog Cuzak following the spoor.

Seconds later, Johan heard automatic gunfire echoing across the valley; Knop must've shot one of the suspects.

Then his radio crackled and a message came through: 'The Warrant is down, the Warrant is down!'

Johan went in the direction he'd heard the gunfire, down a steep embankment.

There he found the ashen-faced constable who'd sent the radio message.

And I saw Peter Knop. He was dead, shot in the head along with Cuzak. I was shocked. I'd known Peter well. He was an extremely efficient member of the dog squad. Now his killers were on the loose with an AK-47.

The chopper was running out of fuel and had to return to base. And the sun was setting. Johan called for back up. It took them more than an hour to get Knop's body out of the gorge.

It was to be a very high-profile case and I led the investigation. We had plenty of leads. We knew that the man we wanted was Mkhize and that he was out to kill policemen. His nickname was Billy the Kid.

Because it was such an emotional case – Peter Knop had been a legend in the dog squad – policemen from other units began hunting for the killers too, hoping to make an arrest. The result was an uncoordinated investigation that often tipped off the suspects and dragged on for more than a year. Johan got irritated and asked head office to send out a circular telling members to butt out.

Despite this, three policemen from the Vehicle Collision Unit of all places, received information that Mkhize was hiding out in Lamontville. Instead of channelling the information to the task team, they went in and tried to flush him out themselves.

What the policemen – Michael Venter, Grant Cummings and Tyrall Samuels – didn't know was that Mkhize himself had phoned radio control and was lying in wait. It was dark, and as the three approached in a marked police car Mkhize opened fire. Samuels was killed instantly, Venter managed to jump out but was shot when he returned to the car to get his firearm, while Cummings fled and hid in a big black rubbish bin. Cummings could hear the killer, armed with an AK-47, tramping about looking for him. He stayed in the bin, not daring to move. At first light he poked his head out, saw that the coast was clear and went for help.

Johan arrived to find a traumatised Cummings – and Venter dead next to the car, his Uzi next to him. Samuels was slumped in the back seat, a gunshot wound to the throat, a cigarette burnt to ashes between his fingers. The killer was long gone.

The image of that cigarette in Samuels' fingers has remained with me – it was poignant. He must've died instantly. Heaven knows how it affected Cummings.

A few days later, on 22 July 1992, Mkhize, accompanied by four men, known to be his bodyguards, went to collect cash takings from a taxi business in Isipingo owned by his mother, ANC stalwart Florence Mkhize. Murder and Robbery detectives, acting on information, spotted him outside the house of the taxi operator, Rashid Khan. A wild shoot-out began.

Mrs Shamim Khan was quoted in Durban's *Daily News*: 'I saw a minibus screech to a stop not far from the house. Men with guns were running, shooting, windows were shattering.'

Cornered in the Khans' house, Mkhize and his gang threw a hand grenade at the police, wounding two of them. Johan raced to the scene: it was a residential area and the situation needed to be carefully managed. His immediate superior, Vlaggies Roux, who had taken over from Leonard Knipe as the commander of Durban Murder and Robbery, was there too.

It was chaos. Sergeant Adrian Ash and a detective – Joseph Chiliza – had shrapnel wounds to their faces and hands. A bullet had struck a water pipe and there was water gushing everywhere. Vlaggies and I took cover down an embankment with a warrant officer called Andy Budke. When the shooting stopped for a bit, I called over to a nearby Casspir and told the driver to park between us and the house.

Shielded by the armoured vehicle, Johan and Budke jumped into the back as the shooting from the house resumed. Johan told the driver, Pine Pienaar, to head straight into the building. Pienaar needed no second invitation and crashed into the wall, knocking it down.

Andy Budke stuck his R5 out of the top of the Casspir and returned fire. When he stopped there was silence. Not a sound. We realised the threat must've been neutralised and did a careful approach.

Sibusiso Mkhize, aka Billy the Kid, only 20 years old, lay dead next to the house. It seemed as if he'd been killed before the heroics with the Casspir. The other four bodies lay in and around the house, riddled with bullets. An unexploded hand grenade lay near one of them.

As word spread that Mkhize had been killed, police from all over Umlazi, 8 kilometres away, arrived to see his body.

Shamim Khan emerged from the house, her thighs and ankles dripping with blood from broken glass.

The *Daily News* reported her saying: 'We spent more than an hour on the floor trying to cover the children who were screaming. It was terrible. Everything in our house is blasted to pieces and so is our car.'

That evening, listening to the radio news playing sound bites of the gunfire, Johan realised what they'd been through. It could've been from any war zone in the world.

Natal was a safer place.

It had been one year and 20 days since the shooting of Peter Knop. He would've been pleased.

But not everyone was. The Mkhizes were a powerful and well-connected ANC family. Many years later it would be proposed that the R603 linking the South Coast to Pietermaritzburg be renamed S'bu Mkhize Drive.

- 3 -

COPS AND ROBBERS

Organised crime, say experts, tends to grow rapidly during periods of political transition, when levels of violence are high. State resources are concentrated in certain areas and gaps emerge in which highly efficient criminal groups find a way to operate.

In the early 90s, scores of well-trained MK operatives were returning to South Africa, with access to Russian weapons. They also had the approval of ANC firebrand Harry Gwala, the 'Lion of the Midlands' who, according to information on the ground, encouraged his followers to fight the old order and commit robberies to get funds to continue the struggle to the ballot box.

Johan found there was a marked difference between the traditional breed of robbers and these hardened returnees.

Your typical armed robber had a fancy house, luxury cars, a cupboard full of leather jackets and a dozen bottles of aftershave. These guys had nothing flashy. But they had AKs and Makarovs and recruited seasoned robbers to provide them with logistical support.

In KZN, armed robberies soared. Increasingly sophisticated anti-theft devices on cars made them more difficult to steal so criminals hijacked vehicles instead. Many of these would be used as getaway vehicles for heists, which were planned to precision, says Johan.

One group would stake out the target, another would execute the robbery, flee the scene and dump the vehicles at a spot where a third group was waiting with getaway cars.

A notebook found in an abandoned getaway car at the time showed that the robbers had even worked out exactly how long it would take a police chopper to reach establishments they'd targeted.

Durban Murder and Robbery's Colonel Vlaggies Roux, a soft-spoken person, began talking tough. He told the *Daily News*: 'The time has come for the police to take off the gloves. We are going to hit back at the robbers with all our might. We are determined to smash these gangs that are terrorising business in KZN.'

Public pressure to fight crime didn't exactly go hand in hand with the new South African focus on human rights and accountability. Johan found it hard to consider human rights when confronted by murderous criminals intent on taking him – and his fellow law enforcement officers – out.

He'd find himself chasing robbers on the wrong side of the N3 freeway one day, leading pre-dawn raids the next, and constantly having to make split-second decisions – sometimes the wrong ones.

Once Peter Bishop and I were doing a stakeout with a team because we'd been tipped off about a robbery. We were keeping an eye on the robbers, who were double-parked outside their intended target. But the Metro police were in the area and told the robbers to move, not knowing they were our suspects. When we saw them pulling off, we followed, ending up on the highway. They saw us, suddenly did a U-turn, and headed straight for us in the fast lane.

Bishop prepared for a collision.

I took off my sunglasses and put my shotgun on the floor. They missed us by an inch and hit a bakkie head on, killing the driver.

Johan reversed so they could arrest the robbers.

But before I knew it we'd been smacked by another police car. I flew across Peter's lap and out of his door, landing on the tar, breaking my shoulder. We both ended up in hospital, as did three of the suspects.

It was a tricky time of transition for a police force that had for years upheld discriminatory apartheid laws. Police officers were, according to the Criminal Procedure Act of 1977, allowed to use deadly force if there was no other way to prevent the escape of a suspected schedule one offender. The law later changed.

•

In March 1992 Johan attended a crime scene in Umlazi where a construction worker had been shot dead. Colleagues from Murder and Robbery followed up and two suspects – Vuzi Nkwanyana and Sandile Khuzwayo – were duly arrested and detained at the Umbilo Police Station. An HMC 9mm sub-machine gun and a .38 revolver were recovered from Nkwanyana, who was also wanted for attempted murder, rape and armed robbery

Three weeks later, Johan got a call from an informer that Nkwanyana had been seen in Isipingo. He'd escaped from custody, but Murder and Robbery hadn't been told.

That night the same informer phoned me at home to say Nkwanyana was in Malagazi, an informal settlement not far from Amanzimtoti. To save time, I asked Willie Olivier, who lived nearby, to go with me, as well as two constables from the Toti police station.

The informer directed them to a house and said Nkwanyana was sitting in a Kombi with several other men. Olivier and Johan saw the vehicle in the road outside and approached from the left. The two constables went to the other side.

The car's sliding door was open and I grabbed Nkwanyana, whom I recognised. He was incredibly strong and wriggled and kicked so that his shirt came off. We eventually got him out of the vehicle and I put an arm around his neck, while Willie held onto his waistband.

Struggling wildly, they edged him towards their car so they could handcuff him, while the constables guarded the other occupants.

Suddenly Nkwanyana punched Johan in the face, stunning him. It felt like his cheekbone was broken. He heard Olivier shouting: *'Fok, Johan, hy's los!'* ('Fuck Johan, he's loose!')

I instinctively fired a shot, then another. He carried on running. I fired three more shots and he fell to the ground. We called an ambulance but by that time he'd already died.

Johan, nursing his aching face, radioed the duty officer for the area. He or she would have to do a shooting incident report, fill in forms and, once the investigation was complete, consider whether the shooting was lawful or not. A detective from the Isipingo Police Station would do the investigation.

In accordance with the Inquest Act, any unnatural death has to be investigated. Police process the scene, take statements, complete ballistics reports and attend the postmortem. Then the docket is sent to the attorney general who decides whether to prosecute. If the AG declines to prosecute, the docket goes to a magistrate to finalise the inquest proceedings.

Johan gave the duty officer his details and went off to the doctor, who filled out a J88 injury form for him. Later that week he and Olivier wrote statements and submitted them, as did the constables who'd been with them. But the investigating officer never took statements from the occupants of the Kombi. Nor did he bother to draw sketches or take photographs. Johan had to find the other men who'd been in the Kombi for him.

Weeks later he contacted me to ask where they could find these witnesses. It wasn't my job to find them – but I didn't want to come across as uncooperative, so I located them.

The incident was considered serious enough to warrant a probe by the Goldstone Commission, which investigated political and criminal violence within the police between 1991 and 1994. The Commission report was scathing about the investigation into the shooting:

> Absolutely no effective investigation was done in this case for three months. An independent Investigation Officer was not appointed immediately. Except for the rudimentary investigation done at the scene of the crime by a uniformed officer who was only conducting an administrative enquiry into the use of firearms, nothing else was done.
>
> The investigating officer should not have relied on a possible suspect, Captain Booysen, to make important witnesses available to him, i.e., the other occupants of the Kombi. He should have traced these witnesses himself.

Johan agreed, but thought if he hadn't told the investigating officer where to find the witnesses he would have been accused of withholding evidence.

It was a case of damned if you do, damned if you don't. As far as I was concerned the Goldstone Report was backing me up. The investigating officer shouldn't have relied on me to trace the witnesses; he should've found them himself. And the Isipingo branch commander should've made sure the investigation was done properly.

•

DAILY NEWS
10 JULY 1992
THREE KILLED IN BATTLE
Detectives from the Murder and Robbery Unit and the Reaction Unit shot and killed three suspects in a fierce 2am gun battle with a gang of heavily armed robbers ... Captain Johan Booysen, who headed today's pre-dawn raid ... said they came under heavy fire ... one of the suspects killed is a member of the ANC who returned recently to South Africa after receiving military training.

Just months after the Nkwanyana incident, members of the Police Reaction Unit were on the tail of a gang linked to two holdups at the Durban Fresh Produce Market. The unit, which provided tactical assistance in high-risk operations, arrested four suspects, who directed them to the rest of their gang who were hiding out in a caravan in Umlazi.

Members of the Reaction Unit went ahead to do a stakeout while Johan, a team from Murder and Robbery and the handcuffed suspects waited in a police minibus.

Having ensured that the suspects were being guarded and reckoning on a long wait, Johan took a nap in the vehicle.

At about 2am I was dozing when all hell broke loose. We could see tracer bullets hitting the fence right near our vehicle. We piled out, including the suspects, pushing and shoving to get out of the same door. It was quite comical, despite the danger. They certainly weren't going to escape with bullets flying. Instead we all jostled for the best place to hide.

A radio message came from the Reaction Unit saying they needed a Zulu speaker.

The gang members, holed up in a caravan on an open piece of land, weren't budging and they wanted to try to talk them out, rather than shoot them out. One of my guys, Ben Paneng, volunteered. He wasn't in the first flush of youth, so I went with him. We leopard-crawled to reach the others.

The robbers weren't interested in what Paneng had to say, firing a few bursts at him – and anyone else who dared lift their heads.

I realised that this could go on all night, so decided to up the ante. I told someone to throw a hand grenade at the caravan.

To their consternation, it didn't explode – and they didn't dare approach in case it did. Instead they called for a Mamba, a small armoured car, from the local police station.

The Reaction Unit approached in the Mamba. The suspects opened fire with an AK-47 and our guys shot back. I saw two bodies on the ground and the hand grenade, which was alarmingly close to a gas bottle. We had to call the Explosives Unit to remove the gas bottle. By the time they'd detonated the grenade the sun was coming up.

A search of the premises netted an AK-47, pistols, F-1 hand grenades and cash. Three suspects were killed, one of them an MK member.

The following year there was another incident involving ex-MK operatives, this time in Durban's Essenwood Road. Increasingly Johan was finding himself at odds with the nearly new order.

To me they were just greedy robbers. Political affiliations were irrelevant – but not to everyone.

Sergeant Mossie Mostert from Durban's Murder and Robbery had received a tip-off about an armed robbery about to happen at the Musgrave Centre on the Berea. The informer had given him the registration number of the suspects' vehicle, a white minibus. Johan phoned the Air Wing to collect him, while two teams set off, one from Murder and Robbery and another from the Reaction Unit. Near Durban High School they drove past an unoccupied minibus fitting the description. As the two teams passed the minibus, they noticed a head pop up and down again.

Peter Bishop was driving one of the police vehicles. He screeched to a halt: 'The Reaction Unit guys driving behind me saw the guy's head too. They were lying on the floor of the vehicle. There was a helluva shoot-out.'

Johan, in the helicopter, heard about the shoot-out on the police radio. He got the pilot to land on the school's sports field and ran across the road.

It was bizarre – five men lying dead right outside the Musgrave Shopping Centre, which in those days was very upmarket. The Reaction Unit had shot them as they emerged from the minibus, armed with automatic rifles.

But an eyewitness told reporters that the men had been shot in cold blood, saying they had been ordered to lie down and were executed on the road. There was an immediate outcry. The ANC demanded that foreign police experts assist in probing the case.

About a week after the shooting the *Daily News* reported: 'The ANC met Natal Attorney General Tim McNally to discuss the removal of the Durban Murder and Robbery Unit from the investigation after learning that Captain Booysen was involved in the killing of an MK cadre last year.'

That MK cadre was S'bu Mkhize – Billy the Kid.

Major Bala Naidoo, spokesman for the Provincial Police Commissioner Chris Serfontein, wrote a letter to the editor:

> Your reporter left out certain important findings of the inquest court. The court concluded that the shooting where the said MK member was killed was found to be justifiable. This MK member was involved in several criminal offences. We emphatically deny that Captain Booysen or any other member of the SAP is involved in a witch-hunt against MK members. The SAP has become the target of a well-orchestrated propaganda campaign.

The Goldstone Commission got involved again. British and French policemen were seconded to the investigating team and an independent ballistics expert examined the bullet-ridden minibus.

At the formal inquest, where witnesses were called to give evidence, the counsel for the families of the dead men, Kessie Naidu, said the men had been targeted because they'd been linked to the killing of a policeman the week before.

But, says Johan, the witness who claimed to have seen the men being shot could not corroborate his account at the inquest.

He burst into tears while being cross-examined by Advocate Gideon Scheltema and said he'd been mistaken. The pathologists concluded that the position of the entry wounds proved that the deceased weren't lying down at the time of the shootings.

In February 1994, Regional Court Magistrate Jimmy Howse ruled that the shootings were justified.

•

To Johan, there were few things more satisfying than good old-fashioned detective work, uncomplicated by politics.

I'm sociable, I like helping ordinary people; I like solving crimes, giving people faith in the police. I don't like worrying about whose toes I'm treading on.

He was on standby duty one evening when a call came through about a murder in Umhlanga Rocks. The uniformed branch was on the scene, but they needed someone from Murder and Robbery.

Johan arrived at an upmarket house in Chartwell Drive to a strange briefing from the local police. Someone had phoned the house to say he had taken the owner, Emily Takis, hostage. She and her husband, André, owned a copper and gift-manufacturing business. There appeared to have been a lot of blood on the floor. Although it had been cleaned up, the grouting on the tiles still had red stains. The domestic worker, Isabel Nxumalo, had been stabbed and tied up by a man who'd gained entry to the premises when she'd arrived at work that morning. He had then hung around the house, eating food from the fridge and drinking beer, until Emily Takis arrived home.

While Johan and detectives searched for clues, the phone rang again.

The same person who'd phoned before told Stompie Ellis, the policeman who answered, that he'd left a letter under the couch. It was a ransom note, demanding R2 million for the return of Mrs Takis.

What the caller didn't know was that police had just found her body in a shallow grave in the garden, under some shrubs.

Johan told Ellis to keep him on the line. He went next door and asked to use a neighbour's phone. It was 1994 – the police hadn't yet been issued with mobile phones.

I called someone I knew at Telkom, gave him the Takis' phone number and asked him to trace the call. The operator said he could only do that if they double clicked the cradle button while the caller was on the other end.

Johan ran back, told Ellis to do the double click and then rushed back to the now bewildered neighbour.

The call was traced to a pay phone at a taxi rank in Umhlanga. Johan got a local patrol car to escort him to the exact location. As he got there a man hastily exited the booth, leaving the phone dangling.

I grabbed him by the belt and searched him. He had American dollars in his pocket and an expensive wristwatch, which I established had been taken from the Takis' house. Although he denied having been there, there was a speck of blood on his sock.

In the first case of its kind in Durban, DNA was used to compare the deceased's blood to the blood on the suspect's sock. It was the evidence Johan needed.

DNA was new to South Africa. It's like a fingerprint and is conclusive, but it's no good unless you have something to compare it with. That spot of blood on his sock placed him at the scene of the murder.

The accused had once worked for Emily Takis and had been fired. So he'd bludgeoned his former employer to death with a crowbar.

•

On 29 January 1995, General George Fivaz was appointed National Commissioner of the new South African Police Service. Gone was the 'Force', with its negative implications.

There was to be no kicking down doors in the new South Africa. Suspects had to know their rights and police had to sign their pocketbooks confirming that the culprit had been advised of them. There were grumbles on the ground that the new Constitution gave criminals too many rights.

When Commander Vlaggies Roux went on extended sick leave, worn down by years of stress, Johan became acting head of the Durban Murder and Robbery Unit.

He was a tough taskmaster, obsessive about punctuality.

I always say that the day I became an officer I didn't enter a popularity contest. I would set my watch to Telkom's talking clock and if members were even a minute late for morning parade at 7.30, they'd be singled out. If you don't have self-discipline you are not going to meet your targets and deadlines and you are not going to listen to the orders of your superiors. Punctuality is as important as rank. When you are out there fighting a war against criminals, someone must take the lead and call the shots. A lack of discipline leads to the breakdown of cohesion, which eventually leads to a dysfunctional unit.

Johan would make sure that everyone on parade was sober – and properly dressed.

I wanted to change the stereotypical view people had of Murder and Robbery detectives. I didn't favour the casual look with a 9mm stuck into the back of jeans. I wanted my detectives to look professional, especially in court, where I expected them to wear a collar and tie.

But Johan realised that discipline wasn't going to win the hearts and minds of the people they were serving. For that to happen, the police needed a new strategy, which was to partner with the public in fighting crime. It was a tall order in a society in which white residential and business areas were well patrolled and within easy reach of police stations, while in townships the police lacked legitimacy and stations were under-resourced with poor service levels.

Johan appealed to the public to come forward with information. Communities that once saw the police as the enemy had to accept them as their partners and protectors.

But then Shobashobane happened – an event that jolted a country basking in the afterglow of rainbow democracy – back to reality.

- 4 -
SHOBASHOBANE

In December 1995, for the first time in his working career, Johan was able to take leave at Christmas. He looked forward to spending time with his family. His oldest son, Morné, would be home from university, the two younger ones, Eben and Natalie, on school holidays.

There had been changes at work. Johan had been promoted to senior superintendent and put in charge of a National Priority Crime Unit. The aim was to create an FBI type of unit, with skilled members selected from Murder and Robbery, Firearm and Vehicle Theft. It would focus on gathering intelligence and infiltrating crime syndicates.

But somehow it never got off the ground and Johan found himself a colonel without a unit.

It was incredibly frustrating. I'd just come from Murder and Robbery, which was high pressure and intense – now I sat at HQ in a collar and tie and attended meetings with commissioners.

The day after Christmas, he was preparing a braai at home when he received a call from Major General Frik Truter at provincial HQ. There had been a massacre at Shobashobane, a rural area near Port Shepstone. The town itself was an ANC-dominated ward, surrounded by IFP zones.

There'd been as many as 500 attacks and counterattacks in Shobashobane since 1990, but overall levels of political violence had dropped dramatically in KwaZulu-Natal in the post-election period.

Recently, ANC youth who had been pushed out of the Shobashobane area had returned and set up self-defence units under the leadership of local chairman Kipha Nyawose. Tensions with IFP members, led by Izingolweni chairman and alleged warlord Sipho Ngcobo, had begun festering. On Christmas Day an IFP hit squad numbering about 600, armed with automatic rifles and traditional weapons, launched a full-scale offensive.

Those on duty at the nearby Izingolweni Police Station were hopelessly ill prepared. Normally there would have been three patrols in the area, but it was Christmas and there were none. It took police four hours to establish control, by which time 18 ANC supporters were dead – shot, stabbed and speared. Nyawose was disembowelled and his genitals were cut off.

Provincial HQ had to do damage control. Truter asked Johan to assemble a team of investigators, which annoyed him.

I had a title and a rank, but no team to call on. And suddenly I had to find one. Most of the local detectives were on holiday. Truter knew this. I decided to go there and assess the situation for myself. He came with me. Things weren't sounding good.

There had been allegations of direct police involvement in the massacre and accusations of collusion, with policemen identified as suspects.

Johan and Truter walked into the Port Shepstone Police Station and introduced themselves to senior officers.

Truter told them I would lead the investigation. They said the witnesses were taking refuge at the Anglican church, but that they hadn't yet taken statements because the community wouldn't let them in.

Accompanied by a lieutenant, Nathaniel Kweyama, Johan walked across the road to St Katherine's Church. The courtyard was crowded with the displaced residents; there were portable toilets in the parking lot and laundry hanging on a jungle gym. A woman pointed at them and started shouting. Lieutenant Kweyama translated: the police were the sons of Satan and they had shot her relatives.

A man approached them. He seemed to have taken charge of the survivors. It was Bheki Cele, an active member of the ANC in KZN. Officially he coordinated security and peace initiatives in the area, but his enemies regarded him as a thug and a gangster. He would, in later years, come to play a very different role in Johan's life as National Police Commissioner. But right now he was breathing fire and telling the witnesses not to cooperate.

Johan wished he were back at his braai.

Cele said the police had been involved in the Shobashobane killings and that they didn't trust us anywhere near the investigation.

Cele didn't stop there. He said he'd warned police of an impending attack, yet all they'd done was to remove weapons from ANC supporters – but when the IFP killers crossed the valley to attack Shobashobane, not a single security force member had been on standby to prevent clashes.

Johan realised that he wasn't going to get anywhere by staying there being blasted by Cele.

I drove back to Durban, assembled 25 of the best detectives I could find from all over the province, many of whom had been on Christmas break, and told them we had to find the killers – without the assistance of the ANC's witnesses.

They went to the local hospital, got statements from those who'd been injured and gathered enough evidence to obtain four warrants of arrest.

One of these was for Sipho Ngcobo, whom eyewitnesses had identified as being part of the massacre. Some alleged he had led the attack. But apparently that wasn't good enough for the politicians.

Newspaper headlines screamed from London to Los Angeles and back.

UK INDEPENDENT
30 DECEMBER 1995
MASSACRE OF ANC VILLAGERS REVIVES SPECTRE OF WHITE EXTREMIST THIRD FORCE

LOS ANGELES TIMES
30 DECEMBER 1995
HOLIDAY ATTACK SYMPTOM OF SA TENSION

MAIL & GUARDIAN
12 JANUARY 1996
POLICE ACCUSED OVER CHRISTMAS DAY MASSACRE

Deputy President Thabo Mbeki, Safety and Security Minister Sydney Mufamadi and National Police Commissioner George Fivaz visited Shobashobane and announced at a media briefing that a national police unit would take charge. The investigation would be led by Johan's old supervisor, Brigadier Bushie Engelbrecht, who had just been appointed head of a new SAPS Special Investigating Unit, intended to deal with high-profile cases countrywide.

Johan was upset that a strong punching arm was being brought in from Pretoria to bolster what the public perceived to be weak policing at regional level.

And he was particularly annoyed that the announcement had been made at a news conference. He demanded to speak to Fivaz, but was told the general was rushing to catch a flight. So Johan sent him a message, threatening to resign unless he was given a chance to explain what his team had achieved and under what circumstances.

Fivaz came over and jokingly asked me why I was giving him a hard time. I gave him a detailed report I had prepared, told him we had identified suspects and asked him to read it. He said he understood, but that the entire affair had become a political hot potato.

Engelbrecht took over Johan's team and brought in more detectives from across the country. In his book *A Christmas to Remember*, Engelbrecht comments:

> When I took over the investigation, some of the detectives from Durban police units became invaluable members of my team ... I met with Colonel Booysen on New Year's Day and he briefed me fully about developments. I decided to make him my second in command and ordered that most of the Durban policemen remain on the team. The fact that some of them could speak Zulu and knew the dynamics of the province was very important to the investigation. Things appeared to be going well until I was told that the local ANC objected to Booysen's being part of the Special Investigation Team.
>
> I refused to withdraw him until they could provide me with a satisfactory explanation as to why he should be removed. A few

days later, however, both Booysen and I were told by Head Office that it would not be in the interests of the investigation to keep him on the team and he was instructed to return to Durban.

Johan assumed the Goldstone Commission inquiries into shootings he'd been involved in hadn't helped his case.

But the main reason was that KZN police were seen as having been complicit at Shobashobane – it didn't matter that I had nothing to do with rural policing at Izingolweni. We were all painted with the same brush.

Four months later, on 18 April 1996, Engelbrecht launched a night raid on Izingolweni called 'Operation Shobashobane' and rounded up the suspects.

Ten months later, on 2 February 1997, the Shobashobane trial began in the Durban High Court. Eighteen accused, among them a 14-year-old boy, were charged with murder.

Only one policeman testified in the trial as a witness for the defence and he was discredited as unreliable. His testimony was an apparent attempt to provide an alibi for the IFP's Sipho Ngcobo who, although sentenced to life, successfully appealed his conviction and was acquitted on all charges relating to the Christmas Day massacre.

Police involvement was never proved in court.

Johan later testified at the subsequent Moerane Commission of Inquiry, which found no evidence of complicity by police management.

•

After Shobashobane, Johan made another mental note to steer away from politics. He would soon come to realise just how impossible that was.

KZN was a very volatile province politically between the general election of 1994 and the local government elections two years later. I was drawn into high-profile cases and many of these had political overtones.

On 25 April 1996, he had a call from Durban area commissioner Bongani Ntanjana, who would, the following year, become KZN's deputy provincial commissioner.

He said there had been an attack on King Goodwill Zwelithini's family residence at Mbelebeleni in KwaMashu. They needed to get there fast. Johan picked him up at HQ and they travelled the 25-odd kilometres to KwaMashu in a police-issue Opel Kadett in less than 20 minutes.

After that Ntanjana nicknamed me 'Bhanoyi' – which means aeroplane in Zulu. He said driving with me was like being in a low-flying plane.

On arrival, the single-storey royal house was in disarray. A gang, armed with spears, machetes, knobkieries and firearms had stormed the premises and attacked members of the royal family as they were about to host a function marking the opening of a township sewing project. Queen Buhle, the King's second wife, was hit over the head; her daughter Sibusile was slashed in the face and shot in the leg. The attackers accused them of 'mixing with communists'.

Missing was the King's first cousin, 35-year-old Princess Nonhlanhla Zulu. A search began. It was assumed she'd been abducted from the royal residence.

Her body was found the following day, in a field adjacent to an IFP-dominated men's hostel, about seven kilometres from Mbelebeleni. She had been stabbed and hacked to death.

The attack on the Royal House in a province wracked by rivalry between the ANC and IFP again made headlines around the world.

NEW YORK TIMES
26 APRIL 1996
ZULU KING'S WIFE WOUNDED IN ATTACK

THE WASHINGTON POST
28 APRIL 1996
BODY OF MURDERED ZULU PRINCESS FOUND

CHICAGO TRIBUNE
28 APRIL 1996
ZULU PRINCESS' SLAYING RAISES TENSION LEVEL

There was pressure on Johan to solve this one fast.

Local government elections were due in less than a month and there needed to be stability in the province. They had already been postponed several times in KZN because of political unrest.

After receiving information that the attackers lived in the hostel near where the princess's body was found, the Priority Crimes and Reaction Units conducted a raid. Johan spoke to journalists afterwards:

'At 5am today we surrounded the building and arrested nine men whom we identified as being part of a gang that attacked the royal residence. We have also seized two guns which are to be sent for ballistic examination.'

That day President Nelson Mandela went to visit the recuperating queen.

'It's clear that a political organisation is involved,' he told reporters outside St Augustine Hospital in Durban, where the queen was listed as being in a stable condition. 'It's not just a question of ordinary crime.'

Johan suspected his days of investigating ordinary crime might have come to an end.

We were about to enter an era in which greed took over from political violence in KZN. It was the era of the big cash robbery and at the forefront was a new breed of sophisticated and organised criminals adept at precision planning – and, in some cases, were being assisted by police.

- 5 -

HIGHWAY HEISTS

By the mid-90s, there were more bank robberies annually than there were days in the year.

Johan was quoted in *The Mercury*:

'We have a good arrest rate in murder cases but unfortunately our arrest rate with armed robbery is unacceptably low ... and it's certainly not from a lack of trying ... our investigations have shown that there is no particular cell or gang responsible for this increase and I believe it goes deeper than socio-economic problems ... perhaps because many of them get away, it provides an incentive.'

The word from National Police Commissioner Fivaz was to step up intelligence and use secret agents so that police were in a position to pre-empt and anticipate. He told journalists at a news briefing: 'We have to infiltrate where there are visible signs that certain persons or groupings are busy with crime-related activities...'

Johan agreed but thought another way to get the bank robbery rate down was to involve the establishments being targeted. Using informers, as Fivaz was suggesting, was good for certain investigations – but not if there were more obvious solutions.

I felt that we instead had to be proactive and find ways to make robberies more difficult to pull off. Banks were too easy a target – brazen robbers could walk through the front doors. They would even hold dummy runs before, working out ways to bypass security. After a robbery they even stole the film from the security cameras as they left.

By now Johan's ex-colleague Peter Bishop had moved to the private sector and they worked together to set up an anti-crime forum with Business Against Crime. Banks agreed to added security measures – guards at the entrance, revolving doors, surveillance cameras and glass partitions between tellers and clients.

One major bank disagreed, reluctant to forego personal contact with customers. But it soon found itself an increased target and upped its security too.

With banks harder to penetrate and with more of them keeping as little cash on the premises as possible, robbers set their sights on the vehicles transporting cash. Johan looked on amazed at the novel ways employed to stop a cash van in its tracks.

They would lay spiky chains across the road, which burst their tyres, or drive straight into them in a big old Mercedes with air bags to protect them during the ensuing collision. On impact, the cash van would invariably fall on its side, giving the criminals access to the safes.

At Colenso, a robber bizarrely clad in a diving suit and crash helmet used a stolen truck to ram a cash vehicle, leaving the truck he was driving virtually obliterated. The robber was killed on impact, despite the supposed protective gear he was wearing. His cohorts grabbed the money and made a vain attempt to free him, but his leg was stuck in the mangled mess.

Soon highway heists also became an everyday occurrence in KZN. When cash transit companies began building sturdier vehicles, robbers upped the ante. They would pour petrol over armoured vans and threaten the guards inside that they would set the vehicles alight unless they gave them access to the cash in the back. By the time Johan and the police arrived on the scene, the robbers had abandoned the trucks and escaped in accompanying getaway cars.

It was becoming apparent that gangs were pooling their expertise and experience to pull off major heists in Gauteng and KZN: the bigger the gang, the better the planning. We couldn't keep up.

The gangs would have a team that specialised in stealing sturdy vehicles to do the ramming, a team that procured firearms, bulletproof jackets, false number plates, angle grinders and getaway cars. They would have safe houses for plotting the heists and for dividing the spoils afterwards. They would do recce-run after recce-run, until they'd planned the crime to perfection. They would target cash vehicles in remote areas so that police response times were slower. And often when the police did have successes, says Johan, they were let down by the courts.

Courts were very liberal in granting bail and suspects would disappear to commit another heist to get money for their legal defence. Unscrupulous police and prosecutors were complicit too – dockets containing original confessions would disappear between police stations and courtrooms.

Johan, now provincial head of the Serious and Violent Crimes Unit in KZN, suspected that gangsters were bribing investigating officers and court officials. But he had no evidence.

I knew it was happening – I'd been told – and I could see in court how cases would come to nothing because vital evidence and statements went missing.

•

But it was the SBV heist in 1996 – the biggest cash heist in South African history at the time – that would become a prime example of how police were complicit in crimes involving big money. It involved five police officers, some inside help and R31.4 million – and years later it would become the subject of a movie, a crime thriller called *31 Million Reasons*, based on a book of the same name by Naresh Veeran.

The heist began shortly before midnight at the depot of cash security company SBV in Pinetown. A gang of balaclava-clad robbers entered through the main entrance, which had been left open for them. One of the gang members patrolled outside in a borrowed police vehicle while the others overpowered a guard and relieved him of his panic button, keys and Luger service pistol. They had an arrangement with a guard inside who opened the control room. The gang subdued the other guards, loaded the loot into two SBV vehicles and made their getaway.

When Johan arrived on the scene in the early hours, the only lead was from a guard in the control room. He said the landline had rung during the robbery. Johan phoned his contact at Telkom, who had helped solve the Emily Takis murder.

I asked if he could find out which numbers had phoned the SBV landline after midnight. Then we applied for a judge's authority to intercept calls from the numbers he gave us. From these intercepts it was established that the stolen money was being stashed at a house in Sea Cow Lake, north of Durban.

Johan gathered a team of officers he could trust and briefed them away from the office. Lately he found himself having to do this more and more, or risk plans being leaked.

We didn't dare discuss the details of an operation at the office because next thing the criminals would be tipped off. More and more often police were accepting money for information.

They set off to raid the house at Sea Cow Lake. Except they got the wrong house – only realising it after they had already forced open the door. After assuring the indignant homeowner that they would pay for damages, they descended on the house next door and questioned the occupant, a woman who denied involvement. Johan knew from the intercepted phone calls that the cash was in the ceiling.

She eventually confessed and made a statement that the money had been brought to her house for safekeeping by a friend of a friend. She said she hadn't known it was the proceeds of a robbery.

Johan lifted Andy Budke, the same officer who'd been with him during the S'bu Mkhize siege, into the ceiling and called the police cameraman over as Budke emerged with black rubbish bags full of bank notes.

We wrapped the money in a blanket and put it in a police car, carefully filming the locking and unlocking of the boot. Money could mysteriously vanish from crime scenes.

He phoned HQ to tell them they'd made a breakthrough and, stash in the back, drove to the Serious and Violent Crimes satellite office in Pinetown. They locked the money inside a walk-in safe, filming all the while.

KZN Provincial Commissioner Chris Serfontein phoned to say he was calling a news conference and needed Johan on hand to answer questions.

DAILY NEWS
23 AUGUST 1996
COPS RECOVER MILLIONS: FIVE ARRESTED AS INVESTIGATORS CLOSE IN ON GANG BEHIND SA'S BIGGEST-EVER ROBBERY

A Durban family has been arrested in connection with a multi-million-rand robbery, reports Deputy News Editor Anil Singh

Commissioner Serfontein said detectives under the direct command of Senior Superintendent Johan Booysen ... had worked tirelessly to make progress in the case ...

... police were not in a position to say how much money had been recovered ...

'Believe me when I say it is millions. We are getting a team from SBV Services in Pretoria to fly down ... and do the counting. The counting will be supervised by police.'

After the briefing, Johan drove back to Serious and Violent Crime in Pinetown. As he walked in, he saw, to his horror, a pile of money in the middle of the floor – an enormous pile, surrounded by members of the police station, wanting to see the proceeds of a crime that had gripped headlines for days.

They'd taken the cash out of the safe – after we'd carefully filmed it being put in there to show that it hadn't been tampered with – and were picking it up and posing for photographs.

He was furious:

With myself for not taking the key to the safe – and with the section commander for allowing it to happen. He said they'd decided to count it. I wasn't impressed and he knew it.

When SBV officials arrived, they counted R5 067 900, but Johan had no way of knowing if it was the exact amount retrieved from the ceiling.

Lloyds of London, SBV's insurer, took civil action to find the remainder of the stolen cash, which totalled around R26 million. The company employed the services of Johan's ex-patrolman, Brian Denny, now a lawyer with Denys Reitz. It was a mutually beneficial arrangement. The police wanted to solve the crime; Lloyd's wanted its millions back.

Johan assigned the case to a team of detectives, including Martin Hall, an unorthodox investigator brought in from the Western Cape.

He wasn't a team player by any stretch of the imagination, but made more progress than anyone else.

Hall had information that a sergeant who called himself 'Cobra', attached to the Chatsworth police station, had been involved. It was common knowledge that Cobra had once shot someone at the police station, but the case hadn't been properly followed up. Hall got a warrant for his arrest and began engaging with him. He eventually turned state witness against his other cop colleagues.

CITY PRESS
25 OCTOBER 1998
MINISTER PRAISES ARREST OF COPS

Safety and Security Minister Sydney Mufamadi and the security firm SBV Services have praised the sleuths who caught senior policemen and former SBV guards this week in connection with the biggest cash-in-transit heist in South African history.

A task team under the command of Captain Martin Hall of the Serious and Violent Crime Unit swooped on two police stations this week and arrested five cops…

The arrest of the cops, who were on duty at the time, follows civil action by SBV insurers Lloyd's of London who are suing 14 people for money still missing.

Over the next two years, an investigation would reveal that millions had been deposited and transferred via a maze of bank accounts and invested in insurance policies. One of the accused, a policeman who earned a monthly salary of R1 500, bought five taxis registered in a family member's name; another paid cash for a new car in R50 notes; one bought a nightclub. Flats were even hired to stash cash.

Sixteen of the 19 accused were found guilty and received sentences of between five and 43 years. But the two arrested at the Sea Cow Lake house were acquitted because of technical flaws in the application by Crime Intelligence to intercept calls. The evidence became fruit of the poisonous tree, rendering it inadmissible – even though it had led the police to millions stashed in the ceiling. It was a lesson to Johan.

It made me exercise much more caution in the future. I realised how important it was to do things by the book – or you would create loopholes for the defence to exploit.

It may have closed the chapter on one of South Africa's biggest and most brazen heists, but there were plenty more waiting in the wings. Often Johan would find himself sending officers from one cash-in-transit crime scene to another on the same day.

Getaway cars would be dumped at various locations, creating secondary crime scenes. Processing a crime scene with a secondary crime scene is very labour intensive – it can take up to five hours. Often while your officers are busy there, the suspects are committing another crime, management is on the phone wanting updates, while the family of the victim is wanting to view the body – and ballistics haven't arrived yet. In some religions they need to bury the body soon after death and you have to explain to shocked and bereaved people why they can't.

Sometimes it was hard to tell if the crooks had gotten away with all the loot, or if some had been left behind and stolen by civilians or the first police officers on the scene.

At a heist near Stanger, a gang of 20 robbers stole more than R10 million but only R320 000 was recovered.

CITY PRESS
15 FEBRUARY 1998
TOP COPS VOW TO BRING SUSPECT POLICE TO BOOK

A top KwaZulu-Natal policeman vowed this week to go on a personal crusade to see that the police said to have stolen part of the R10.2-million cash-in-transit heist on the North Coast two weeks ago are put behind bars.

Senior Superintendent Johan Booysen, commander of the KwaZulu-Natal Serious and Violent Crimes Unit, made his commitment after rumours surfaced that some members of the province's Murder and Robbery Unit took some of the loot.

'At the moment I know nothing except that speculation and

rumours were doing the rounds this week. This is an unsubstantiated story, which the media has made a fuss about. But I vow to see to it that when the person who claims to have witnessed the heist makes a statement to the police, I will personally investigate the matter and bring the culprits to book,' he said.

Johan was frustrated. Robbers were becoming more brazen, police more crooked and the court system more corruptible.

At a heist at Gingindlovu, southwest of Richards Bay, where robbers made off with R7 million, using a stolen truck, detectives found a cash slip issued that day from a garage south of Mooi River. Johan phoned a colonel in Pietermaritzburg.

I asked him to go to the garage and check the CCTV camera footage recorded at the time the receipt was issued. He phoned a few hours later to say the truck in the footage matched the one at the scene and that the driver was talking to the occupants of a car. The number plate of the car was clearly visible.

A check of the car showed that it had a tracker and was travelling past Heidelberg towards Johannesburg. The suspects were apprehended in Soweto that night. But they got off – another police success marred by bungling in court that got Johan's blood boiling. He began formulating a plan.

I needed to somehow get rid of the bad apples. We couldn't carry on risking our lives then have the suspects get off in court because police may have been paid to compromise cases.

Most of the cash-in-transit heists occurred in the operational precinct of Cato Manor, a run-down urban area five kilometres west of Durban, and were handled by a specialist team based there. But some members had been caught out: for hiding dockets, tipping off suspects in exchange for cash and stealing from crime scenes. Johan decided he needed to do something.

I took a decision that would have a ripple effect later in my career. I decided to create a task team within a unit.

Those who wanted to be part of it would have to undergo a polygraph test. Simple, straightforward questions:

Have you ever compromised an investigation by taking money?

Have you ever assisted robbers in getting away?

Have you ever lied in court?

Have you ever stolen an item from a crime scene?

The new team was selected. They drove BMWs and Chev Luminas and had all the latest equipment, allocated to them by the provincial commissioner. The impression was that they were an elite squad that was well looked after.

All Johan wanted was the job done by a team that wouldn't let him down.

Obviously there was jealousy and plenty of muttering. But our mandate was to fight crime – and we needed the best people to do that. There was competition to belong to the Unit.

The team members would later come to be known by their detractors as 'Booysen's Blue-Eyed Boys' – the Cato Manor Serious and Violent Crimes Unit.

- 6 -
CATO MANOR

Between 1996 and 2006 the national police service was reorganised. Highly specialised units were closed and taken down to station level, with the intention of strengthening the capability of police in crime-ridden areas. Only three specialised units were retained: Organised Crime, Serious and Violent Crime and Commercial Crime. It was a model adopted successfully in some countries overseas with local police chiefs being given power over their own precincts. Johan didn't think it would suit the short-on-skills South African scenario, but got shouted down when he voiced his opinion at a meeting of top brass.

The problem with shoving together disparate units is that skills and knowledge get watered down. We needed strong and independent specialised units dedicated to tackling corruption and criminality. But many of the people making the decisions had no experience – one of the generals even thought that police stations should deal with cash-in-transit heists. The idea was preposterous and I told her so.

Johan's post as senior superintendent was upgraded and he became director of Serious and Violent Crime (SVC) in KZN. More than 400 police officers were now under his command from a dozen disbanded units throughout the province.

I had to get them into teams so that members complemented each other and so that even the weakest members performed specific functions effectively.

In 2006 things changed again. Serious and Violent Crime merged with Organised Crime, including Narcotics, Endangered Species, Vehicle Theft, and Diamond and Gold Units, with Johan as overall provincial commander. He had to try to develop the same passion towards fighting poaching and contraband as he had for investigating violent crime. He needed to learn the lingo and a whole new police sub-culture.

I went on a narcotics course with the German Bundeskriminalamt and I was fortunate to have Lieutenant Colonel André Laatz at head office with me. He'd spent his entire career doing narcotics investigations so I relied on him to manage the drug investigations in the province. I knew I couldn't work in isolation – I consulted widely with officers who were experts in their fields.

There were Organised Crime units at Richards Bay, Port Shepstone, Pietermaritzburg and Durban. The Cato Manor Serious and Violent Crimes Unit became a sub-section of Durban Organised Crime and covered an area from Tongaat in the north, Karridene near Umkomaas in the south and stretched as far west as Botha's Hill. The members combined their skills and developed a huge database of suspects. Each member had a specific function. There were docket carriers, who obtained witness statements, forensic evidence and confessions from the accused and prepared dockets for trial; field workers, who gathered intelligence and tracked suspects; and data analysts, who focused on bank statements and cellphone records. It was, thought Johan, exactly the kind of unit KZN needed to reduce crime levels by penetrating syndicates and acting on tip-offs.

One thing they all had in abundance was human intelligence: information sourced from informers, people on the ground. They were energetic and passionate about their work.

Johan's old friend Willie Olivier was placed in charge of the 40-member Cato Manor sub-section. They cracked cases station-level detectives were unable to; they seldom compromised crime scenes or lost court cases. Olivier collected numerous awards for excellence on behalf of the squad. Olivier comments:

> We would work 24- and 48-hour shifts to get the suspect; sleep in our vehicles, sleep in the bush if we had to. On any given day

we'd attend two or three robberies and an ATM bombing. After eight months we brought that number down to one incident a day, by smashing syndicates. We would not go home until we'd solved a case – complicated cases, with lots of interference from suspects via their contacts in SAPS.

Each Organised Crime Unit had a commander. Colonel Rajen Aiyer, respected by few of his colleagues judging by the number of complaints received about him, was unit commander of Durban Organised Crime. Olivier, as commander of the Cato Manor sub-section, was obliged to keep Aiyer informed when there was action going down, but they all considered him a hazard on an operation.

Aiyer wasn't Johan's favourite person either.

He once tried to get a cleaner to falsely accuse me of racism. The cleaner refused and sent someone to tell me to be careful of Colonel Aiyer. I got the cleaner to submit an affidavit and opened a file on Aiyer. It didn't take long before it was full. His own brother, someone from his son's school, the family of a murder victim, the local prosecutor's office, his co-workers, you name it, they all had complaints.

In 2003, Aiyer told a superintendent at KZN HQ that Johan, together with the IFP and several other police officers, was plotting to assassinate Mpumalanga Provincial Commissioner Eric Nkabinde.

Nkabinde had once been stationed in KZN and he and Johan had been close.

Alarmed, the superintendent, Sipho Mbele, compiled a written statement for Crime Intelligence:

> I was very much perturbed about the information and a few days thereafter I asked Colonel Aiyer whether the information he relayed to me was true and he reiterated what he told me previously ... I do not have even the slightest doubt as to the integrity of the officers who are implicated ... I have known Director Booysen since his school days ... he and Commissioner Nkabinde regard each other as father and son.

Johan suspected that the reason KZN police management had never acted against Aiyer, who had committed indiscretion after indiscretion, was because he was known to have the ear of National Police Commissioner Jackie Selebi. He had apparently impressed Selebi with his struggle credentials, his family having provided refuge to Albert Luthuli in Groutville in 1964. The ANC chief had held little Rajen in his arms.

'I was the only child Luthuli carried,' Aiyer told anyone who would listen.

So-called struggle credentials or not, Johan considered Aiyer a dangerous information peddler. He believed he was promoted at the expense of loyal and dedicated police members.

But I had enough to do without worrying about Aiyer's pathetic attempts to destroy my career. There were 62 cash-in-transit heists between 2005 and 2006 in KZN alone. The most notorious route was the N2 between Durban and Swaziland.

•

Early on 3 October 2006, Johan got a call from Organised Crime at Richards Bay. There had been a heist – two Fidelity Security trucks had been hit – and the robbers were heading towards Durban, tailed by the Flying Squad.

Soon, the investigating team would discover that the day before, a tactical route planner for Fidelity, Themba Sithole, while driving to work at 3.30am from his home in Eshowe to his office in Richards Bay had noticed four cars – two of them BMWs – travelling in convoy.

Although it was dark, he could see that each vehicle contained four or more men. He remembered that a few weeks before, a similar BMW had been used in an attempted heist. He noted the number plates and followed the convoy to Richards Bay and into an area called Mzingazi, where the four cars parked outside a house and the occupants of the vehicles went inside. Sithole phoned the Richards Bay police, but was told they couldn't assist because they were changing shifts. He phoned again. This time two officers arrived, but when they realised how big the gang was, they said they needed back up. They disappeared and never returned.

Sithole finally gave up and went to his office. It was 7.30am. But he couldn't rest. He had a feeling a robbery was being planned. He told Fidelity investigator Kevin Govender, who phoned a policeman he knew in Richards Bay to be on the lookout.

That evening, two Fidelity cash-in-transit vehicles, travelling 30 kilometres apart, were ambushed and overturned on the N2.

Both vehicles had spent the day collecting money from businesses in northern KZN. The drivers had been heading back to base in pouring rain when one of them saw what looked like a police roadblock ahead. The driver of the first vehicle slowed down and was rammed by a speeding 7-series BMW. The other cash van – some way back – was hit by a Mercedes. While making their getaway, the gang killed a security guard, shot at other motorists and hijacked a vehicle, abducting the daughter of a local councillor. In the mayhem they left behind R350 000 in cash. As they fled, a policeman who happened to be passing saw the fleeing robbers and shot and injured one of them.

When Sithole heard there'd been a heist he went to the scene. He recognised the bashed and abandoned BMW and the Mercedes as among the cars he'd seen early that morning. He told his colleague Kevin Govender, who was there with a captain from Richards Bay Organised Crime, that these were the cars he'd spotted and that he knew where their base was. Sithole took them to the Mzingazi house, where they waited for something to happen. At about 10pm between 30 and 40 males got into three vehicles, one of them a white Kombi. The captain told the Empangeni Flying Squad to meet them en route and they followed the cars. The best place to confront them would be the Mvoti toll plaza, south of Stanger. The Durban Flying Squad would provide back up once they got there.

Johan arranged for Cato Manor to be on standby to take charge of the investigation.

I prefer specialists to do it: if the perpetrators aren't properly linked to all of the crime scenes, they'll walk free. The Locard principle is the theory that when two objects come into contact with each other, one will always leave a trace of itself on the other: the perpetrator will bring something onto the crime scene and leave with something from it. Whatever those things are can be used as forensic evidence, but the investigator needs to work out what they are. Not every police officer can do that. The Cato Manor team knew exactly how to properly process a crime scene and the importance of it. They would spend hours there, and afterwards be able to narrow down the pool of suspects.

A stickler for proper crime scene management, Johan had lectured on the topic at detective courses.

I always tell the story of Watson asking Sherlock Holmes: 'What are you looking for?' Holmes answers: 'I don't know, but I will when I find it.' You won't find it unless there's proper crime scene management protocol in place. The crime scene needs to be cordoned off because there are so many ways that it can be contaminated and the integrity compromised. Even smells are important – that's called transient evidence – things like aftershave, cigars, sweat, curry or perfume – things that can tell you something about the victim and the perpetrator.

But that morning they didn't need to hunt for clues.

At midnight, a petrol tanker pulled up to one of the two tollgates that were open. The driver was alarmed to be bundled out of his vehicle by a Flying Squad member. With the tanker blocking the lane, there was only one tollgate available for the Kombi of robbers to use. As they pulled up, three Flying Squad members, armed with assault rifles and handguns, surrounded them. The driver, who would become accused number 24, got out first, his hands in the air.

The other 13 occupants were ordered out and ten more suspects were rounded up from the two vehicles following behind. They had on them two AK-47s, one LM5 and a shotgun. There was a petrol-operated angle grinder in one of their cars.

When Johan got there, 24 alleged robbers were lying on their stomachs, their wrists bound with cable ties.

There were fat wads of cash everywhere – in their cars, in their pockets, in their pants. They were like mobile ATMs – someone joked that if you swiped a bankcard through their bum cheeks, money would've poured out.

As dawn broke and KZN residents began their day, the investigators and their suspects were still at the toll plaza. One of the first vehicles to pull up was a school bus, full of children. They hung out of the windows and cheered the police when they saw the handcuffed gang, who would become known as the 'KZN 26'.

At the Mzingazi house, which belonged to accused number 24, Mbuso

Mncube, police found moneybags and banking receipts from Fidelity clients. Despite this, Johan doubted they had enough evidence.

While there were lots of exhibits, there was little actual evidence. Traces of paint on the angle grinder didn't match either of the Fidelity vehicles, so clearly the gang hadn't used it. Although illegal, the firearms found in the Kombi still had to be sent for ballistic examination. The most the suspects could be charged with was the illegal possession of firearms.

One of the AK-47s was eventually linked by ballistics, but most of the money was missing. Probably on its way to Joburg, Johan thought, in the pockets of the gang members who hadn't been arrested.

The money found on the 26 arrested robbers – R51 000 here, R35 000 there – wasn't marked. So that didn't help the investigators either. We decided to get a cellphone analyst to try to link the gang members to one another.

Thereza Botha, a clerk from Vryheid SAPS, was appointed to do the analysis. She had helped to crack a case in Vryheid linking multiple murders to two perpetrators through stolen phones and swapped sim cards.

Organised, sharp and determined, Botha set about analysing 72 000 phone calls made by the KZN 26. Between September and October 2006 the accused had phoned one another an abnormal number of times. By comparing their cellphone contacts and communication patterns, she was able to link the 26 accused to a wider gang and discovered that, on the day of the heist, calls were made and received via the Richards Bay lighthouse phone tower, near the Mzingazi hideout. It was painstaking and pernickety work and Johan knew they had to tread carefully.

I was mindful of the intercepted calls that had been thrown out as evidence in the SBV case. We had to follow up whatever information we got from the cellphone analysis with proper investigation.

The investigating officer, Lieutenant Colonel Eddie van Rensburg, got a tip-off that the robber who had been shot, who would become accused number 25, was in hospital. Kalanga Ubisi's blood matched some found at one of the crime scenes.

A bullet had lodged in his back. But doctors said they couldn't remove it to test it because it was in a dangerous spot behind his shoulder. They needed to wait until it had worked its way out naturally.

Eight months later, Van Rensburg checked Ubisi out of prison for an X-ray. Doctors said the bullet was now near the surface and they would remove it the following day. Van Rensburg would finally have his evidence. That night, in his cell, Ubisi removed the bullet himself with a sharpened spoon and flushed it away.

But Botha's cellphone analysis had been able to place Ubisi at the scene of the crime – and at the hospital. His cellphone records had literally signposted his trip to the Prince Mshiyeni Hospital, near the Durban Airport cellphone tower. On the way one of the other accused had called him six times.

The trial began in October 2007 and was a massive affair: 26 accused, 31 charges each. It lasted four and a half years and was held in the High Court sitting at Pongola. The main challenge, says Johan, was to keep them in custody.

Many of them were out on bail already and had come from Joburg to commit the crime. We managed to oppose bail for all but one, who was then linked to another heist and his bail was revoked.

At first they were detained in special cells on the seventh floor at Durban Westville Prison. Only Van Rensburg and the suspects' lawyers were meant to have access to them. But information was leaked that they had been smuggled phones and a firearm, and were planning an escape by staging a hostage situation when they got to court. The gang members who hadn't been arrested had obtained passports for those in custody so that they could flee across the Swazi border from Pongola. A search of the cells at Westville unearthed a firearm in a drainpipe.

The KZN 26 were relocated to Kokstad C-Max, a maximum-security prison usually reserved for sentenced prisoners who were a flight risk. When the trial began they were moved to the Pongola police cells during the week. Van Rensburg made sure he controlled access to the cells and handpicked the guards. On a Sunday afternoon before court the following day, a team from Tactical Response and Public Order Policing would fetch them to avoid any dramatic liberation attempts between Kokstad and Pongola.

There were no security lapses during the trial. For every court appearance until they were sentenced in 2012, the accused were paired at their ankles in thick chains and guarded by heavily armed police officers placed at different points in the courtroom.

In his judgment before giving them life sentences, Justice Jan Combrinck said:

> What makes this trial somewhat unique is the introduction of wide-ranging and detailed cellphone evidence … 72 000 calls were analysed … and what we find heartening … was the thoroughness and commendable competence with which the arrests, search and collection and recording of exhibits were carried out … by the Organised Crime Unit at Cato Manor, Durban. The professionalism displayed at the scene of arrest is of the highest order, more so, given the extremely difficult circumstances in which the police had to work.

For Johan, the final chapter in one of the country's biggest criminal trials was a satisfying one. Cash-in-transit robberies had decreased dramatically in KwaZulu-Natal.

- 7 -

THE ASSASSINATION OF LIEUTENANT COLONEL CHONCO

On 27 August 2008, Johan was on a course in Pretoria when he received a call that Lieutenant Colonel Zethembe Chonco, who coordinated taxi violence investigations in KZN, had been assassinated.

Johan didn't know it then but it would be the Chonco assassination that would have the most profound effect on his career, eventually leading to the closure of the Cato Manor Unit and the arrest of most of its members – and himself.

In the middle of a lecture, I excused myself and headed back to Durban. I knew Chonco well; he was often at head office. Although quiet and unassuming, he had an appetite for investigating taxi violence.

Chonco had been station commissioner at Kranskop in the Tugela Valley, a hotbed of taxi violence. Some of the most prominent taxi empires hailed from there: the Sitholes, the Mkhizes, the Mchunus, the Gcabas and Big Ben Ntuli, said to carry three pistols on his person and several shotguns in his car. Legend has it he would hire a helicopter as his transport to avoid being taken out. Ironically, in the end a mosquito got him – he contracted malaria while on the run in Swaziland.

The KZN government had been trying to get a grip on taxi violence for a decade. As Transport MEC S'bu Ndebele told a taxi prayer meeting at the University of Zululand in 1999: 'We have not worked so hard to end political violence only to have it transferred to the taxi industry.'

Taxi operators seemed motivated by two things: greed and revenge. Hitmen – known as *'izinkabi'* – were hired to settle scores and sort out those who poached lucrative routes: R100 000 a hit, depending on the status of the victim. Some taxi associations had security companies on a retainer who provided the triggermen.

Chonco had tried to bring warring taxi associations together to talk peace, an unrewarding and relentless task. There would be consensus around a table one minute, shooting at a rank the next.

Johan had had his fair share of the taxi underworld.

Back in February 1996, he and Olivier had investigated the shooting of 69-year-old taxi boss Simon Gcaba inside an ice-cream parlour in Durban. The killing, allegedly ordered by Big Ben Ntuli, had sparked a bloody war. Johan and Olivier were warned by KZN Crime Intelligence to watch their backs. Olivier imagined *izinkabi* lying in wait for him at his home. At the gym with his wife, he saw from the second-floor window suspicious characters lurking outside near his car. As he walked down the stairs, hoping to avoid them, he saw a man with an AK-47. Olivier froze.

> *Inkabi* always wait until a target gets into his vehicle and shoot him through the front windscreen. I've seen it happen so many times and now I saw it happening to me. These guys were standing three metres away from me. I 'klapped a toon' – I ran. My wife didn't know what was going on. I flagged down a car and got a lift to Johan's house and shouted: 'Sparrie – that's what I call him – they are here for us!' He got his R5 and we went looking for them, but they were gone. Later we heard they had gone to Ladysmith to take out some rivals and had been taken out themselves. Investigating the taxi industry isn't a job you want in the police.

It wasn't a job Johan wanted either: he thought it a crime-prevention function. There were thousands of illegal taxis operating lucrative routes.

Police should be checking permits and doing regular searches for illegal weapons. Nonetheless, he'd found himself sucked into a Transport Violence Committee at the behest of his bosses and ended up chairing it.

We would discuss the same things without making real progress; nobody seemed to want peace in the taxi industry. For every killing there was a counter killing. No matter what we did, it was wrong. If someone was arrested, then you were accused of siding with a rival association; if you didn't arrest anyone then you were accused of not being committed.

After the killing of 11 people at a taxi rank in Empangeni in November 1999, an inquiry was set up. Both Johan and Chonco testified at the Alexander Commission. Chonco told the Commission: 'We have had star witnesses who saw an attack and have taken strong statements from them. Later, we heard they had changed their allegiance to another taxi group because of intimidation. Or we would hear that witnesses were dead.'

Commission chairman, Judge Gerald Alexander, identified delays in bringing suspects to court and police complicity as contributing factors. When Johan became a commissioned officer, even his wife's employer had to meet management approval. She couldn't, for example, work at a liquor store, regarded as a place of ill repute. But 15 years on, every third policeman seemed to have an uncle, cousin or brother in the taxi business.

In 2007 Chonco was instructed by Provincial Commissioner Hamilton Ngidi to take charge of solving taxi violence – through intelligence gathering and reactive investigation. Conflict resolution on the ground and enforcing legislation on taxi routes had proved ineffectual.

At the time of his death, he had been investigating the Stanger-based KwaMaphumulo Taxi Association, headed by the notorious Bongani Mkhize. Mkhize had numerous brushes with the law, from arrests for fraud and driving without a licence, to murder and attempted murder.

In 2004 it was alleged Mkhize had been shooting at a taxi owner, a police informer, from the passenger seat of his Mercedes when his driver hit a teenage girl at the side of the road. She was killed and four other people were shot and wounded, including the intended target and his family. The case was withdrawn when the taxi owner, as well as Mkhize's driver who was to be a state witness, were shot dead. Police suspected Mkhize's involvement. That same year he was arrested in connection with another drive-by shooting; he was released when those witnesses mysteriously vanished.

Mkhize operated lucrative routes between Stanger and Durban and as far south as Lusikisiki, generating an income of about R30 000 a week. He had a personal bodyguard from a security company and his right-hand man was his nephew, Swayo Mkhize. Swayo was out on bail for murder, but the witnesses kept disappearing – an effective way of assuring that cases never got to court.

Chonco had been waiting for evidence to put Swayo away. Just recently there had been another hit and there were plenty of people who saw Swayo do it – too many for even him to get rid of.

On 24 August 2008, Swayo appeared in the Pietermaritzburg court in connection with an old murder case. As he emerged, still out on bail, Chonco was waiting on the steps to rearrest him. Swayo realised he was in serious trouble. One of the people he had shot in the latest incident had survived and could identify him. It was unlikely he would get bail again. The taxi underworld feared what would come out at his trial. While Swayo was supposedly being kept under heavy guard in a cell at the Kranskop Police Station, a detainee in the same cell overheard Swayo making plans to escape en route to court. He got word to Chonco's brother, a policeman who was stationed at Kranskop, and he told him to watch out.

On the morning Swayo was due to appear in the KwaDukuza court, Chonco was hyper-vigilant. He organised a three-car convoy to transport his prize prisoner. What he didn't know was that a cellphone had been smuggled to Swayo and he had texted their movements from the back of the police van.

The route had a detour because of road works. It was classic ambush territory. The *izinkabi* lay in wait. Chonco's convoy slowed down as it approached the detour. They allowed two police cars to pass then sprayed AK-47 and R5 bullets at Chonco's car. Despite being critically wounded, Chonco's colleague, who was in the passenger seat, returned fire and killed one of the *inkabi*. The others fled, leaving Swayo still locked in the back of the police van.

Chonco was killed behind the steering wheel of his car, his jaw obliterated by an AK-47 bullet, which had emerged from the top of his head.

Commissioner Ngidi wanted immediate action. He had brought Chonco on board to solve taxi violence. Now he was dead and taxi thugs were terrorising the province. Ngidi seldom went to crime scenes, but he flew to this one by helicopter with his deputy commissioners, Fannie Masemola and Bongani Ntanjana.

Cato Manor detective Mossie Mostert was already there.

It was shocking. An AK-47 bullet wound isn't pretty. Colonel Chonco lay slumped over the steering wheel, smartly dressed for court in his shirt and tie – now covered in blood. The windscreen was peppered with bullet holes. One of his attackers lay dead on the ground, AK between his legs. On his wrist was a bracelet made of goatskin.

While standing near the dead attacker, Mostert heard a phone ring. It stopped then started again – and again. It was coming from the leather jacket on the dead attacker.

'I thought: bingo! I found the phone in his pocket. It would ring for hours and would turn out to be very useful to the investigation.'

When Johan got back to Durban, he went straight to the Cato Manor offices, where Olivier briefed him.

They told me they had made an early breakthrough. They had found the dead attacker's cellphone. His name was Ndlovu. By tracing the calls, Crime Intelligence managed to establish who was there with him.

Thereza Botha, who had worked on the KZN 26 case, did the analysis. She noted that Ndlovu's calls had been routed through two towers – at Nyamazane Hill – 3 kilometres from the crime scene, and Ndaba Farm – just 700 metres away.

A man called Li Buthelezi had phoned Ndlovu 14 times on the morning of Chonco's murder. His last calls had gone unanswered and been routed via the Ndaba Farm tower. Buthelezi had been very close by. He had also phoned a man called Nathi Mthembu multiple times on that same morning. The first call had been at 5:04am from Nyamazane Hill and later shifted to the Ndaba Farm tower. Meanwhile, Mthembu's cellphone records showed that his calls on that morning had also gone via the two towers close to Chonco's murder. He had phoned Li Buthelezi and a man called Khopha Ntuli multiple times. And in the month leading up to Chonco's murder, Mthembu had phoned Ntuli 210 times. Ntuli in turn had been in contact with Li Buthelezi and Ndlovu on the day of the murder from the two closest towers.

All the men had been in communication with a taxi boss by the name of Magojela Ndimande on the day of Chonco's murder, while they were still in the area. They had also been in contact with Bongani Mkhize. Mthembu had made 42 calls to Mkhize in the month leading up to and immediately after the Chonco shooting. Mkhize had phoned the Kranskop Police Station the night before the murder. But Mkhize hadn't been placed near the scene.

The fact that there had been calls made to him by suspects who were close to the scene didn't directly link him to Chonco's murder.

Within 24 hours, the investigating team had names and began bringing other suspects in for questioning. Not in the gentlest of ways, according to some of them. Jimmy Howse, the magistrate who had presided over the Essenwood Road inquest, was now an advocate and was representing Swayo. He phoned Johan to complain.

Howse said that Cato Manor officers had 'illegally' booked out Swayo Mkhize from Stanger police cells, where he'd been placed after Chonco's killing. He'd been interrogated and assaulted at Cato Manor offices.

Johan gave Jimmy an earful, accusing him of living off blood money, while police officers were being killed.

I was upset about Chonco, now I had to listen to complaints after hours about his clients being assaulted.

A taxi security guard called Moses Dlamini, called in for questioning in connection with Chonco's killing, had also made allegations of torture by Cato Manor detectives. He belonged to the security company used by the KwaMaphumulo Taxi Association. He said in affidavit:

> On the 28th August I was taken to Cato Manor Organised Crime Unit … several police officers there … started interrogating me about Supt Chonco's death … then they started assaulting me. My head was covered in a plastic bag, which was used to suffocate me.

They slapped me with clenched fists and kicked me all over insisting that I knew how Chonco died ... as they were busy assaulting me they pulled out a piece of paper and they compared what was on my cellphone book with a list of people they were looking for. They asked me what connections I had with Mr Mkhize.

Johan wasn't there and has no idea if there was torture or not, but he was confident that they had the right suspects. As well as relying on information from informers, investigators had made use of sophisticated tracking methods that enabled cellphones to be located by picking up the identity number assigned to a sim card. Called a 'grabber', the device acts as a virtual cellphone mast and forces signals to route through it instead of the nearest mast. It can be placed in a vehicle to get close to targeted cellphones.

Once the suspects had been identified, the grabber was used to locate some of them, so we knew where they were when it came to arresting them.

On 3 September, four officers, including Mostert from Cato Manor, went to arrest Li Buthelezi, one of the suspects, in connection with Chonco's murder. An informer had told them he was staying at a rented house in KwaDukuza (formerly known as Stanger). They kicked down the door and found Buthelezi in bed with his wife.

Mostert says Buthelezi went to an adjacent room and put on a pair of jeans – then took a pistol from a black canvas bag and pointed it at him: 'I fired in his direction fearing for my life and that of my colleagues. He died on the spot with the firearm still in his hand.'

Buthelezi's wife told investigating officers a different story. She said police had assaulted her and her husband, whom she said was unarmed. The police watchdog, the Independent Complaints Directorate (ICD), was called to the scene, as is the case with every killing involving the police.

But Johan says the ICD investigations was left wanting.

In this case the ICD didn't reconstruct the scene with a ballistics expert, didn't follow up on Buthelezi's landlord's claims that the windows were usually open so there would've been no need to kick down the door, nor did it register a case of assault regarding the wife's claims.

Four years later the Cato Manor officers would be charged with the murder of Li Buthelezi and housebreaking with intent to commit murder.

But at Chonco's memorial service – held on the same day that Buthelezi was killed – Provincial Commissioner Ngidi praised the police, telling mourners at the service they were closing in on the remaining suspects.

'We already know who they are,' he said to thunderous applause.

That night, in an unrelated incident, another senior policeman was killed. Superintendent Frans Bothma had stopped to search a suspicious-looking car in KwaMashu when one of the occupants opened fire, shooting him in the head with an AK-47.

Community Safety and Liaison MEC Bheki Cele said in a statement: 'It is clear that thugs have declared war on police and we will not take it lying down.'

Regarded as a power broker for the ANC in KZN, Cele, who was appointed MEC in 2004, was flashy, flamboyant, formidable and hands-on. He paid surprise visits to under-performing police stations and voiced concern when the station commissioners were nowhere to be found, when police vehicles were out of service, when cells were dirty and unkempt and when he found the occurrence book hadn't been looked at in weeks. He certainly cared when police officers were killed:

SOWETAN
4 SEPTEMBER 2008
ANOTHER TOP COP DIES IN AMBUSH

Outraged MEC Bheki Cele has urged police officers not to die with guns in their holsters but 'to shoot to kill' criminals.

This was after another senior KwaZulu-Natal cop was killed in the line of duty, bringing to two the number of top crime fighters killed in six days.

… Superintendent Frans Bothma, 44, was shot and killed in KwaMashu's K-section at about 7pm on Tuesday during a crime prevention operation.

A statement issued by Cele's department yesterday said Bothma's killing followed the 'orchestrated killing' last week of one of the province's senior officers, Superintendent Zethembe Chonco.

Now every cop in KZN was fired up to find Chonco and Bothma's killers. Two Dog Unit members patrolling in Mthunzini picked up taxi boss Magojela Ndimande and his bodyguard, Tembe, after finding them with guns and cash. A Cato Manor officer who was in the area went to question them; the firearms were legit and they had an explanation as to why they were carrying so much cash. Only when the officer got back to Cato Manor HQ did he realise that Ndimande was linked to Chonco's murder. He phoned and told him to come in for questioning. Ndimande said he would, but never pitched.

On 5 September, lawyers for the KwaMaphumulo Taxi Association served the SAPS with a legal letter, calling on them to stop illegally detaining its members: 'Snr Supt Chonco's murder (which appears to have been exacerbated by the more recent murder of Supt Bothma) does not justify the abandonment of the rule of law and individual rights …'

Everyone questioned in connection with Chonco's death, the lawyers claimed, had been assaulted, Magojela and Tembe being the latest. They requested that any further questioning of KwaMaphumulo Taxi Association members be done in their presence.

The letter was faxed to Johan's direct supervisor, Pat Brown, the provincial head of detectives. Brown sent the letter to the ICD and the SAPS' legal department responded to it, asking for sworn statements from the complainants.

At this point, Provincial Commissioner Ngidi ordered the Chonco case to be moved from Cato Manor to the Port Shepstone Organised Crime Unit, even though some Cato Manor detectives remained on the case. Crime Intelligence suspected a leak – they believed that Ndimande had been tipped off and that's why he had disappeared.

On 16 September, Johan received a call from a highly placed source with a crucial tip-off in the Chonco investigation. Later, some would allege that the source was Cele – but the two hardly knew one another at the time.

While the Chonco killing had thrust Johan squarely into the Cele camp, Johan's first encounter with him had been the hostile one at Shobashobane in late 1995. The second time was years later, with Commissioner Ngidi, when they had briefed the MEC at his

Pietermaritzburg office about what was being done to combat violent crime in the province. Johan had told Cele the only way to get on top of it was to have specialised units.

He agreed and it was clear from his utterances that he supported us. We needed dedicated units to deal with violent crime. You couldn't pussyfoot around murderous criminals.

In fact, the Chonco investigation tip-off didn't come from Cele, but from someone closely connected to soon-to-be Safety and Security Minister Nathi Mthethwa. The source had told Johan that Magojela Ndimande was hiding out in the Free State. That day he would be driving to Pietermaritzburg with his bodyguard, Tembe, to collect cash. Johan alerted the investigators.

Crime Intelligence organised for a surveillance unit to trace Magojela's car, a Hyundai Tucson. It was spotted in Pietermaritzburg. Cato Manor was an hour away, Port Shepstone two hours, so Cato Manor officers took over from the surveillance unit. They were to arrest Ndimande and bring him in for questioning.

Mossie Mostert says he was driving an unmarked car with blue lights when he spotted the Hyundai on the N3. He says he activated his siren, indicating for the Hyundai to stop. It didn't, so the chase began. Close to Merrivale, near Howick, he says Tembe opened the back door and shot at them. Cato Manor Unit detectives in a second car returned fire and Tembe fell out. His foot got stuck and he was dragged for several metres before the car stopped. According to Mostert's statement:

> The vehicle veered towards the yellow line and came to a standstill. I immediately alighted from my vehicle and proceeded towards the driver-side door. I opened the door and noticed the driver, Magojela Ndimande, still had a pistol clutched in his hand. I fired a shot towards him, hitting him in the upper body area. He dropped the firearm … I found an AK-47 in the left back side of the vehicle …

Johan was in his office when he got a call from Willie Olivier to say there'd been a shoot-out.

I phoned the SAPS Air Wing to find out if there was a chopper to fly us to the scene. There wasn't, but there was one on its way back to base and it could meet us there. The pilot, Refilwe Ledwaba, didn't even cut the engines – me and Willie got in – and headed for Merrivale. The N3 was backed up for kilometres and the northbound lane was closed. We landed on the highway 90 minutes after the shooting.

Three years later, in the first of a series of articles on the Cato Manor Organised Crime Unit, *Sunday Times* detailed a very different scenario in a front-page article with the screaming headline: *The Death Squads.*

The newspaper quoted an unnamed source: 'There was no shoot-out. The okes pulled up alongside the Hyundai and just executed them.' The article continued: 'Minutes later, Booysen himself landed in a police chopper.'

The *Sunday Independent* would, on 16 August 2015, quote a 'confidential document': 'Booysen and Warrant Officer "Oliver Willem Cornelius" [*sic*] arrived at the scene in a helicopter and allegedly tampered with the crime scene by placing an AK-47 rifle on their victims to create the impression the deceased were armed and/or would have used it to shoot at the police.'

Rubbish, says Johan.

I got off the chopper with an AK then planted it at the crime scene with dozens of people and half of KZN's journalists looking on?

But on the day after the N3 shoot-out in 2009, that wasn't how top cops in the province saw the incident.

In a 17 September article headlined 'End of the Road for Cop Killers', *The Witness* noted that 'police in KZN seem to be heeding the recent call of Safety and Community Liaison MEC Bheki Cele to defend themselves and "shoot hard at criminals."'

Cele was quoted in another article:

THE MERCURY
17 SEPTEMBER 2008
FAST-DRAW POLICE GET HIGH PRAISE

Bheki Cele commended the work of the police in tracking down the suspects in Chonco's murder. 'The shooting of these criminals shows that police are heeding my plea to shoot at criminals... I hope this will be a lesson to other criminals that police are serious about their work and will not hesitate to protect themselves and the community they serve,' he said.

Three weeks after Chonco's assassination, five people – all connected to the KwaMaphumulo Taxi Association – had been killed in shoot-outs with the police. And they weren't the last.

Unaware of the cellphone analysis that linked them all, taxi boss Mkhize was convinced Organised Crime had obtained a list of names from an informer whom he believed was former Cato Manor detective and traditional leader Inkosi Mbongeleni Zondi.

According to a written confession later made by his nephew Swayo, Mkhize's information was that Magojela Ndimande had been shot on the N3 after meeting with Zondi in Pietermaritzburg and that it must have been Zondi who had tipped off the police.

Mkhize feared he was next. In an October 2008 affidavit, he said that taxi security guard Moses Dlamini had told him that he was on the Cato Manor 'hit list' – something he said investigators had said to Dlamini while they were interrogating him: 'He further cautioned me to be absolutely careful as it appeared that my name generated the most vexation amongst the police...'

Bongani Mkhize's lawyers took an unusual step – on his behalf they applied for an interim interdict, a Rule Nisi, which provides a safeguard for a particular period, citing as respondents the National Minister of Safety and Security Nathi Mthethwa; Community Safety and Liaison MEC Bheki Cele; Provincial Commissioner Hamilton Ngidi, as well as Johan.

> I approach this Honourable Court on an urgent basis... to ensure that my life is not threatened or harmed. I have offered to hand myself over to the ... investigating team under controlled circumstances and in the presence of my legal representatives...
> I believe that if I was approached by the police in circumstances under which my colleagues were approached, I would most definitely be killed.

It was a tactical manoeuvre to put the police off guard – and probably because he was desperately afraid that there was a hit out for him.

> All the people whose names appeared on the list ... have since been killed by the Police. It was alleged that they were arrested for the murder of Supt Chonco and were killed while allegedly threatening members of the SAPS ... All of these deaths have occurred under questionable and suspicious circumstances and I have been reliably informed by certain members of SAPS ... that the policy being adopted by the investigating team is to kill or eliminate all members of my Association suspected of involvement in the murder of Supt Chonco.

In his reply, Johan said Mkhize wasn't a suspect, nor had a warrant of arrest been issued for him.

He said there was no hit list.

The information received from Moses Dlamini is hearsay ... I deny the existence of any list that is referred to by the Applicant ...

Mkhize and SAPS reached an agreement and the final order stated that police could not 'unlawfully kill, intimidate or harass' him.

It was a meaningless and nebulous interdict, Johan thought.

It would later be interpreted that Mkhize could not be killed at all, whatever he did – even if he shot at the police. Surely that would be an act of self-defence on the police's part? Years later it would be used against me to suit a very particular agenda: an agenda that had nothing to do with the lawful or unlawful death of Bongani Mkhize.

He says Mkhize didn't become a suspect until the death months later of Inkosi Zondi – who happened to be the great-grandson of Inkosi Bambatha kaMancinza, who led a Zulu rebellion against British rule in 1906.

We had the phone calls from suspects that pointed a finger at Mkhize, but more evidence was needed to pull him in for questioning. The Zondi case would provide that evidence.

•

On 22 January 2009, Zondi was killed while visiting family members in Umlazi, his car sprayed with AK-47 gunfire. Apart from being of royal ancestry, he was a relative of President Jacob Zuma, who said at Zondi's funeral: 'It is a bitter irony that Nondaba, being a former top detective in the Murder and Robbery Unit would lose his own life in this manner. We appeal for calm and restraint. Let the law enforcement agencies deal with the investigations and track down the killers, and bring them before the law.'

Provincial Commissioner Ngidi insisted that Johan – who had known Zondi – personally handle the crime scene. It was a top-priority case, says Johan.

Although he was a Zulu chief, Zondi had also once been a detective based at Cato Manor but had been transferred years before to KwaMakutha and had been off sick for a year. At this stage I was unaware that the Zondi case had anything to do with the Chonco killing.

The day in January when Zondi was killed was blazing hot in Umlazi. Johan had the area swept with brooms and got labourers to cut the grass. They found dozens of AK-47 bullet casings.

The breakthrough came when the getaway car was recovered. A fingerprint showed that Swayo Mkhize had been in the car – the same Swayo who was being transported to court when Chonco was killed, but who had once again been given bail by the courts.

Cato Manor officers went to arrest Swayo and he spilled the beans in a statement. He told police how Bongani Mkhize and several other men – among them Magojela Ndimande's brother and nephew, Badumile and Sifiso – had met at Steers in Durban North and hatched a plan to kill Zondi for 'selling out' Ndimande. Swayo said that Mkhize's KwaMaphumulo Taxi Association had put forward R150 000 for the operation. Now, because of Swayo's confession, Bongani Mkhize was wanted for questioning about the death of Inkosi Zondi.

•

One morning in early February the same contact linked to Nathi Mthethwa, who had told Johan about the whereabouts of Magojela

Ndimande, phoned to tell him that Mkhize was hiding out in a flat in Ridge Road in Durban.

Bongani Mkhize had been linked to the death of Inkosi Zondi, a relative of the president. Now a close connection to the Minister of Safety and Security was telling me where the suspect was. Naturally I alerted the investigating team and asked them to bring him in for questioning. Along with the NIU they waited for Mkhize in the area.

Cato Manor officers RC Maharaj, Paddy Padayachee, Raymond Lee and Adriaan Stoltz and three members of the National Intervention Unit (NIU) who were used in high-risk situations – Sandile Mfene, Thomas Dlamuka and Sibongile Sikhulume – waited on Ridge Road. Two hours later Bongani Mkhize was spotted in his black Toyota Lexus. When he realised he was being followed, he increased his speed, said the detectives pursuing him.

Constable Raymond Lee: I managed to pull along the right side of the Lexus, the driver's window was down …

Inspector Adriaan Stoltz: I produced my police appointment certificate and instructed the driver of the Lexus to stop … the suspect then produced a firearm …

Constable Raymond Lee: I hit the brakes and pulled in behind the Lexus. It accelerated going onto the right hand side of the road … the driver ignored red robots and climbed pavements to try get away … the suspect then turned right onto Umgeni Road, ignoring the red robots …

Inspector Adriaan Stoltz: I fired several shots at the left and right tyres of the Lexus. The vehicle slowed down and stopped opposite the BP Garage in Umgeni Road …

Constable Raymond Lee: The vehicle containing Tactical Intervention Unit members pulled up along side the Lexus and shots were fired …

Constable Sandile Mfene: The suspect produced a firearm and fired shots in our direction. I, with Inspector Dlamuka, returned fire in the direction of the suspect.

Bongani Mkhize lay dead in his car on Umgeni Road, slumped over the steering wheel. He had been shot nine times.

A police report said the NIU had fired the fatal shots to his head and neck and that there'd been no witnesses.

On 26 August 2012 the *Sunday Times*, in the fourth of a series of articles on Cato Manor, reported that a witness had seen 'a tall Indian policeman' walk up to Mkhize's car and 'shoot him at point-blank range'. There were only two Indian policemen at the scene – RC Maharaj and Paddy Padayachee – neither of them tall at 1.67 and 1.7 metres, but both from Cato Manor, whose members were to be charged with racketeering.

Johan was to face the same charges.

- 8 -

CELE, MDLULI AND THE GROUND COVERAGE REPORT

'Nobody is going to shoot an SA police officer and go and sleep at home. I am referring to the Bible. If you take an eye from us, we will take an eye from you ... If you take a tooth from us, we will take a tooth from you ... There is no New Testament in South African policing.'
– Bheki Cele, *Mail & Guardian*, 12 January 2011

In July 2009 Bheki Cele succeeded Jackie Selebi as national police commissioner. By then Selebi had been charged with corruption, following an investigation by the Scorpions. He had played no small part in the dissolution of the elite crime-fighting unit attached to the National Prosecuting Authority, which was replaced by the Directorate of Priority Crime Investigation (DPCI) – known as the Hawks – which reported to the SAPS.

By late 2009 Johan was being interviewed for the job of head of the Hawks in KZN, and the following year was appointed, becoming a deputy provincial commissioner at the same time. Shortly after assuming the position he went with Provincial Commissioner Ngidi's successor,

Mmamonnye Ngobeni, to Cele's home in Umhlanga Rocks to attend to what Ngobeni said was a 'crisis'. Johan's impression was that Ngobeni was over-reacting; she seemed to be in awe of Cele. When they arrived at his residence, they found nothing untoward: Cele wasn't home, only an elderly woman, two guards and no crisis.

Still, in June 2010, the *Mail & Guardian* reported that Johan had investigated a theft of millions from Cele's home and that it was being kept 'under the radar'; Johan suspected that a faction within Crime Intelligence was behind the newspaper report, which continued:

> The *M&G*'s sources claimed the theft was being investigated by deputy provincial commissioner Johan Booysen, but this week he denied knowledge of the alleged incident: 'It's the first I hear of it.'
>
> Sources in Durban said Cele had made several trips to Booysen's office in recent weeks: 'Booysen is the chief's right hand man,' said one.
>
> Booysen, also provincial head of the Directorate of Priority Crime Investigation (the Hawks), is regarded as extremely close to Cele. His organised crime unit has played a controversial role in investigating violence between rival taxi bodies in KZN.

Johan says he barely knew Cele.

I had no relationship with him to speak of. I'd never even picked up the phone to call him. He hadn't been on the selection panel for the Hawks job. At that stage we'd never met alone, ever. Yet 'sources' said I was Cele's right-hand man. And contrary to this report, Organised Crime hadn't investigated taxi violence since 2006.

The first time they met alone was in Cele's Pretoria office in 2011. Johan had asked for an urgent meeting after someone in Crime Intelligence had given him what he thought was a top-secret intelligence report, alleging corruption and political intrigue in KZN.

The 'Ground Coverage Intelligence Report' had 'SECRET' written in bold on every one of its 20-odd pages.

It accused Human Settlements Minister Tokyo Sexwale and KZN Premier Zweli Mkhize of being part of a group plotting to unseat President Zuma with the backing of the American CIA. The 'Mvela' group also planned to topple Blade Nzimande and Gwede Mantashe, said the report. Several pages of the document were devoted to Bheki Cele: allegations about his office romances, his acceptance of envelopes containing 'thick wads of cash' and his mutually beneficial friendship with a flashy Durban couple Shauwn and S'bu Mpisane, who had made millions in tenders from the KZN government. (Coincidentally Shauwn was the sister of S'bu Mkhize – Billy the Kid.)

The report seemed a crude and convoluted cut-and-paste account of actual events mixed with innuendo, conjecture and blatant lies:

> Cele set the ball rolling to have Supt Chonco from Kranskop shot and killed because he had stumbled on Cele's involvement in the taxi violence in KZN. Cele allegedly organised the hitmen to follow Chonco and kill him … the instruction was that none of the persons involved in killing Chonco must live to talk.

Johan thought what came next was the most scurrilous of all.

According to the report Bheki Cele had Chonco killed because Chonco had discovered that Cele was on the payroll of a taxi association. Cele had used Bongani Mkhize's izinkabi *to do the job then Cato Manor had got rid of them – and Mkhize.*

Johan had given the orders, the 'intelligence' report maintained: 'The head of Serious and Violent Crime, now Deputy Provincial Commissioner and Head of Hawks, is alleged to have ensured this.'

Furthermore, it went on, it was Cele who had phoned Johan to tell him that Magojela Ndimande, wanted for Chonco's death, would be travelling on the N3 that day.

> Cele uses police officials from Organised Crime to eliminate people who are a problem to him … He ensured the appointment of General Johan Booysen who enjoys a healthy relationship with him and carries out his bidding … Sources are confident that Cele acts as the Head of the Mafia in the Province and should any one try to go against him they are taken out or they mysteriously disappear or have an accident …

Johan handed Cele the report. The police chief glanced at it, then said: 'You're too late. I saw it months ago. It's the work of Crime Intelligence and Richard Mdluli.'

Johan felt embarrassed.

I'd flown all the way from Durban to Pretoria, made an appointment with him – and it turned out to be disinformation he was aware of. It had actually been in the newspapers in various guises, but I was oblivious to it and the machinations involving Richard Mdluli.

Crime Intelligence had replaced the old Security Branch and was commanded by Lieutenant General Richard Mdluli, who had once been a member of the Security Branch on the East Rand in the 80s. In the new South Africa, he'd been in charge of the Vosloorus detective branch. While stationed there it was alleged that he'd ordered the murder of the husband of an ex-girlfriend. Yet he had moved up the ranks to become the head of Crime Intelligence and was said to have extraordinary powers. He apparently had more dirt on top politicians than anyone else.

But his past would finally catch up with him.

In March 2011 a warrant would be issued for Mdluli's arrest, on charges of murder, intimidation, kidnapping, assault and defeating the ends of justice.

Following Mdluli's suspension in May 2011, members of Crime Intelligence came forward about the alleged abuse of a Secret Service account. They said Mdluli had used the secret fund like a personal bank account and allowed others to as well.

Mdluli said at the time that the murder and fraud charges were part of a racist-driven plot against him by white police officers.

Colonel Kobus Roelofse of the Hawks had investigated the secret fund abuse and discovered that the head of procurement at Crime Intelligence had allegedly bought two BMWs with police funds, one for Mdluli, another for his wife, Theresa Lyons, who was employed as an undercover agent, despite her having no experience. According to Roelofse's report, she also had a Crime Intelligence Mercedes registered in her name and had accompanied Mdluli on a trip to Singapore, business class, all courtesy of the secret fund.

A number of other senior Crime Intelligence officers and their wives and girlfriends were being investigated for acquiring safe houses, properties, and luxury cars from the fund. Lieutenant General Manoko Nchwe had an Audi Q7 meant for covert operations registered in her name. According to an investigating officer, when the scandal became public she panicked, gave the keys to a Crime Intelligence official and resigned before she could be suspended.

Even Police Minister Nathi Mthethwa had benefited. In 2012 the Auditor-General found that a wall built around his private home in northern KZN to the tune of R200 000 had been paid for from the secret service fund, but that the minister had been unaware of the source of the funding.

Cele told Johan that Richard Mdluli had approached him to stop the investigations.

Cele had refused. Next thing the Ground Coverage Report was doing the rounds, compiled by Colonel NH Singh from Crime Intelligence, also allegedly a beneficiary of the secret fund.

In a statement issued by the Department of Human Settlements in May 2011, Tokyo Sexwale would respond: 'The report is a fabrication ... it is a fake ... the rumour has an author and return address and his office is located within the headquarters of our National Police Department – Lt Gen Mdluli, head of Crime Intelligence Division ... I am informed that we have not seen the last of these dirty tricks ...'

Although Mduli had signed the report, it was only after it had been thoroughly discredited that he claimed his signature had been forged. 'That ground intelligence report is bullshit. It never came from me,' he told the *Mail & Guardian*.

He claimed a senior politician had 'sourced' it.

Whoever was behind it, it marked the start of a major rift in the SAPS, says Johan.

Some of the allegations in the document would become the central theme in an orchestrated drive to discredit those seen as opposed to the Mdluli faction. It was a rift in which crime fighting would be perceived, in the eyes of ordinary South Africans and police members, to be of lesser importance than power and politics.

Brigadier Simon Madonsela – a close friend of Johan whom he had worked with at Organised Crime – was appointed to investigate the KZN beneficiaries of the slush fund. He kept Johan abreast of what was uncovered.

Midway through his investigation, Madonsela was told by HQ to hand in his dockets, all 15 of them. He said he'd been told it was no longer a police investigation, but that the inspector general of Crime Intelligence would deal with it. I suspected they realised that shit was on the way and they needed to rein in the investigators before they found out too much.

After three months, Crime Intelligence Inspector General Faith Radebe returned the original dockets and Madonsela tried to resume his investigation. But he encountered resistance and complained bitterly to Johan, who advised him to subpoena the documents he needed.

Clearly elements within Crime Intelligence had something to hide because they blocked Madonsela at every turn. After he'd obtained the 205 subpoenas and just before warrants of arrest could be issued, he was pulled off the case and it was handed to an inexperienced captain.

Three years later Robert McBride, as head of the Independent Police Investigative Directorate, followed up on the investigation, asking Johan for assistance in obtaining the KZN dockets in order to investigate Mdluli. So Johan enlisted the help of Madonsela, who obtained copies from the investigating officer who'd taken over from him. But when Johan read them he realised they had been sanitised. All incriminating evidence against Mdluli and his cohorts had been removed.

- 9 -

PROVINCIAL COMMISSIONER LIEUTENANT GENERAL NGOBENI AND THE CONNECTED BUSINESSMAN

In late 2009 the newly appointed Lieutenant General Mmamonnye Ngobeni arrived at KZN HQ from Ulundi, a rural backwater with a population of 20 000, to fill the position as top cop in the province. Ngidi had retired.

The dynamics of crime in Ulundi were somewhat different to Durban. By all accounts, expectations there were low, police stations under-resourced and punctuality a foreign concept. To say that the new commissioner was out of her depth would be an understatement, in Johan's opinion.

I missed Ngidi – he'd been a wise and approachable disciplinarian. The new commissioner seemed just the opposite. It had nothing to do with her being a woman, as she would later accuse me of having had against her. It was because I had doubts she was up to the job. I felt that her background and experience were not suited to her current position.

It annoyed Johan that the first thing she did was to change the morning meeting time from 7.30am to 8am – then still had trouble arriving on time. Her staff officer was at her Umhlanga house at 7am, but she was never ready. Yet once her meetings began, they seemed never-ending. Johan wanted to get his day going; he thought the new PC seemed to prefer being sedentary for hours on end. He tried to make the new situation work for him, advising her where he could and maintaining his independence. She overlooked his occasional absences at her meetings, but remonstrated with other officers if they didn't pitch or arrived later than her. So he held his tongue. She didn't cramp his style or interfere with his investigations. Not yet anyway.

She soon learnt that one of the tricks of good management is getting competent people to do the work. She tended to rely on me. If children were struck by lightning in some or other rural area, she'd tell me to get a police helicopter to take me there to investigate. If there was a taxi shoot-out, she'd want me on the scene. I did what she asked of me, but I didn't respect her.

There was a good support structure at provincial HQ: most people were on top of their game. Brigadier Lawrence Kemp headed SAPS Financial Services. He was an old-school policeman who followed treasury regulations to the letter. He'd been provincial finance head for 17 years – he had the Public Finance Management Act at his fingertips and kept an eagle eye on under- and over-expenditure. It was his job to keep the PC informed of any irregularities. She was, after all, the chief accounting officer, even if she did things that made Johan wonder where her priorities lay.

She replaced her office furniture with white leather and had the bathroom redone with brand-new fittings. There was nothing wrong with the old furniture or fittings, and given the constraints of our budget, I thought it was unnecessary. She even brought her own secretary from Ulundi and promoted her to lieutenant colonel without her having done a single exam to qualify.

Johan thought she had the head of Supply Chain Management, Colonel Navin Madhoe, at her beck and call. Johan didn't trust Madhoe. When he had needed new blinds for his office because his were falling apart, Madhoe had wanted him to sign an invoice in excess of R26 000.

I made inquiries and found perfectly serviceable office blinds for R6 000. I suspected Madhoe had an uncle in the furniture business.

There were a few other things about the new PC that seemed slightly off to Johan. Once, when she'd needed personal legal advice, he had referred her to his attorney, Carl van der Merwe, an ex-cop. He arranged to meet General Ngobeni at the Elangeni Hotel and arrived after her. Van der Merwe, a teetotaller, was surprised when, once the PC had left, he was presented with a bill for two double whiskies.

One day, in April 2010, Kemp came to a meeting looking worried, and told Johan he'd found some discrepancies at Supply Chain Management. Astronomical expenditure had been posted against several travel and subsistence items: much higher than normal amounts were charged for accommodation. What alarmed him further was that over the previous eight months contracts for almost all supplies needed by the police in the run-up to the FIFA World Cup had gone to one company, or subsidiaries of it.

That company was Gold Coast Trading, owned by Durban businessman Thoshan Panday.

Panday was in his late thirties, debonair, stylish, and claimed to turn over R60 million a month, trading in diamonds and precious metals. *City Press* once described him as having 'balls of titanium'. He was a director of 22 companies: from precious metal dealing and diamonds to energy and financial planning. He owned a fleet of fast cars – an Aston Martin, a Ferrari and a Lamborghini. According to a company search, his business associates included a Zuma cousin, Deebo Mzobe.

It seemed that a lot of money was coming to him via SAPS Supply Chain Management. Panday had secured a R15-million deal for Gold Coast Trading to provide accommodation – at high prices – for KZN police officers on duty during the upcoming World Cup. Also included in the deal, according to Kemp, were TV sets for police stations, blankets for cells and a generator for R90 000 when it shouldn't have cost anything near that amount.

Johan had never heard of Gold Coast Trading or Thoshan Panday. He asked the provincial commander of Commercial Crime to initiate an investigation and two colonels – Vasan Subramoney and Hans van Loggerenberg – were appointed to look at Kemp's report. They got from Kemp the file and banking details of two officers working at Supply Chain Management – Navin Madhoe and Aswin Narainpershad – who, they suspected, were responsible for ensuring that Panday was used above anyone else as a broker for police supplies, accommodation and travel.

They also obtained Section 205 subpoenas to access Panday's bank accounts, and discovered that Madhoe and Narainpershad had spent weekends away with their families at Panday's expense and received gifts like a second-hand car and a brand-new treadmill.

In return, 'emergency' or 'urgent' situations were created to benefit Panday. Madhoe would write the necessary memos, for 'the professional service rendered to the SAPS on short notices, to date', for the accommodation of police members.

DEPLOYMENT OF SAPS MEMBERS TO CRIME 'HOT SPOTS'
ESTCOURT

Initial request was received on 2009-12-04 with the deployment period being on the same day. Due to the urgency of the request and the short time frame only one service provider Goldcoast Trading was approached for assistance.

NONGOMA

Initial request on 2009-10-29 for deployment the same day for 8 members. Only one quote was obtained from Gold Coast Trading as it was impractical to obtain more quotes.

NDWEDWE

Initial request received on 2010-01-08 for 54 members. Only one quote was obtained from Goldcoast trading as this was during peak time as well as short notice.

Kind regards
Section head: Acquisition Management
N MADHOE

And so it went on. Cheaper quotes from other companies were ignored in favour of Gold Coast. Sometimes Panday's companies bid against one another to give the appearance of a competitive process. In this way, he had so far been paid out R45 million from KZN Supply Chain Management.

About a week after the procurement investigation began Johan was driving home when he got a call from Ngobeni saying he should stop it immediately.

She said there was enough going on in the province. She gave the example of the Mountain Rise Police Station, near Pietermaritzburg, which was being probed for manipulating stats, as well as the theft of IT equipment and televisions. She said another internal investigation could be embarrassing for SAPS. I told her it would be more embarrassing if we didn't investigate.

A few days later, Johan got a call from her PA. The PC wanted to see him.

I knew something was up. It had just gone 7am. She never came to work so early.

When he got to her office she wasn't alone. With her were Deputy Provincial Commissioners Bongani Ntanjana and Fannie Masemola, as well as Brigadier Kemp and Colonel Madhoe.

The PC looked distinctly unhappy, her arms folded, her lips pursed in a coat-hanger shape Johan knew all too well.

Madhoe was looking smug, Kemp perplexed. He wasn't a feisty character and had a gentle manner. General Ngobeni launched into him, accusing him of being more concerned with saving money than saving lives.

Kemp tried to explain the abnormally high charges to her and said that he was in the process of compiling information for head office about it.

This really set her off; she was furious that he had informed the national SAPS office. She told him direct lines of communication with head office must stop immediately.

Johan assumed Ngobeni was expecting him to say something because she kept looking at him. He decided to hold his tongue.

Things were getting heated: Kemp was upset and she was furious. I didn't agree with her, but as one of her deputy commissioners I didn't want to say anything in front of junior officers, so I asked her if Madhoe and Kemp could be excused.

When they'd gone and he and the other two deputies remained, he explained the severity of the situation: an internal report indicated that all KZN SAPS supplies were being channelled through one company.

Treasury regulations were being shrewdly side-stepped by keeping quotes low enough to avoid a tender process and by listing contracts as 'emergencies'. We could hardly ignore it. Not only was it unlawful, it would have a negative impact on the provincial budget.

PC Ngobeni opened a tin of snuff, took two quick snorts, sneezed into a tissue and told Johan to hand over the file.

General Ntanjana could do an internal inquiry. Procurement and Supply Chain Management fell under him.

Johan knew Ntanjana didn't have the staff, or the wherewithal, to conduct such an investigation. To appease Ngobeni he retrieved the file from Colonel Subramoney, but didn't give it to Ntanjana.

I knew there was more to the matter and I decided to sit on it until I'd figured it out.

Subramoney got suspicious and without telling Johan emailed General Anwa Dramat, national head of the Hawks, and told him that he thought Johan was blocking his investigation. Subramoney would write in a subsequent affidavit: 'I briefed Dramat about what had ensued ... he indicated that I had his support and must continue with my investigation.'

Johan kept the file in his office, only to have the PC phoning him up on one Saturday in a panic because she'd heard the investigation was continuing. She shrieked at him: 'What is wrong with your people?'

Johan wondered what was wrong with her. He'd never known her so interested in an investigation. He assured her he'd instructed investigators to stop the probe into Panday.

Meanwhile Subramoney thought that Johan was protecting Ngobeni. His investigation was going nowhere, as his later affidavit explained: 'I encountered fierce resistance from officers in the province. They were either too scared to speak to me, or those who did were called in and reprimanded.'

Subramoney had found out that Panday had been paid R236 000 for accommodation meant to cost R63 000 and that Panday had paid for a rental car for Major General Ravi Pillay, who worked at Supply Chain Management's national office and wielded significant influence in the final stages of contract approval. Panday's phone records showed that he was in regular direct contact with police officers in KZN and national procurement. He'd once, according to a forensic audit report, even phoned a company claiming to be 'an agent of SAPS National head office'.

Crime Intelligence reported that Panday had also approached Captain Kevin Stephen in the police deployment division. In an affidavit made much later, Stephen would say the two met in a private suite at a cricket match and when Panday had heard where he worked, he'd suggested they cook up something together. Stephen said Panday had told him to register a company.

Johan was at a conference in Pretoria on May 19 when Dramat approached him and asked why he was blocking the Panday investigation.

I told him the provincial commissioner had ordered me to. Dramat said I should continue. I should bypass provincial police structures and instead report to Serious Economic Offences in Pretoria. I now felt justified in ignoring PC Ngobeni's repeated instructions to stop the investigation.

But he still wanted to prove to her how serious it was.

I decided that once I had sufficient evidence, I would send both her and General Ntanjana a preliminary report. But then I heard something that made me realise what was going on. PC Ngobeni also appeared to be on the Panday backhander list.

The Hawks had figured out that Panday had also paid R20 000 for a party for Ngobeni's husband, Brigadier Lucas Ngobeni, at the upmarket Dish restaurant in Umhlanga on 29 May. He imagined how it had happened: maybe Colonel Madhoe, concerned that a new broom could scupper some of his moneymaking schemes, had suggested to her that Panday would be able to finance the party.

Perhaps Madhoe made it sound perfectly legit, as if this was a regular thing – business people sponsoring members of the police, no strings attached. But when word got out there was an investigation, Madhoe must have told her to watch out. Panday wanted his quid pro quo.

Although the party hit the headlines in 2011, the SAPS investigation stretched over years, culminating in Ngobeni's suspension in 2016. In 2014 she told journalists that she had asked a team in her office to arrange the birthday event. They'd come up with a list of service providers, she explained, and Thoshan Panday's company had been selected to 'handle the party'. She hadn't even known who he was, she said. 'I only knew Panday after the allegations that he had paid for the event. He never paid for the event. He was paid for his service and I have an invoice to prove that,' she told the *Daily News*.

But Johan thought she had known exactly who Panday was. He had sent her and General Ntanjana a report, detailing the extent of the corruption and the identities of the suspects. Two weeks later, on 22 June 2010, she had summoned him to her office.

Without a word she took me to her boardroom and there, to my amazement, was Panday and what looked like an army of advocates. I felt as if I'd walked into an ambush.

Panday – a small man – was immaculate in a pinstriped suit and red tie. He asked Johan why Subramoney had been checking his bank accounts without a Section 205 subpoena. Half of Johan thought: *'Who is this little twit?'* The other half wondered how on earth he'd found out. Who had leaked? The bank, a magistrate, someone on the investigating team?

It was as if Panday had read the report he'd given Ngobeni and Ntanjana.

I told them it would be foolish of Subramoney to conduct such an investigation without a 205. Then they accused him of trying to extort money from Panday to stop the investigation. It was clearly an attempt to discredit Subramoney as an investigator.

Johan could scarcely believe it when the PC instructed him to stop investigating Panday and start investigating Subramoney instead.

I asked for proof of the extortion attempt from Panday, which one of his lawyers agreed to supply. It came a few days later in the form of a written statement, saying Panday had received an anonymous call asking him for a million rand to make the case disappear. It wasn't proof at all. Nonetheless I was ordered to open a docket against Subramoney.

•

A week after the Panday meeting, on 28 June 2010, Johan received a

Johan and his mother, Makkie, at a school athletics day, 1972. (Personal collection)

Riot squad duty in 1978 in Lamontville, south Durban, with Willie Olivier second from the left and Johan in the middle. (Personal collection)

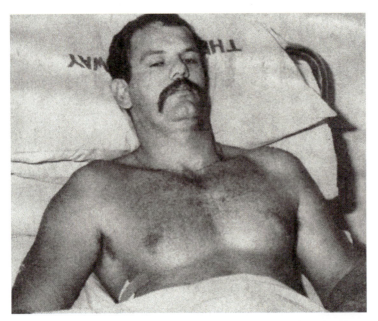

Johan in hospital after the Umbumbulu attack in 1986. (*The Daily News*, edited by Gerhard de Bruin)

Isipingo shoot-out in 1992, during which cop-killer S'bu Mkhize was slain. (Richard Shorey/ *The Daily News*, edited by Gerhard de Bruin)

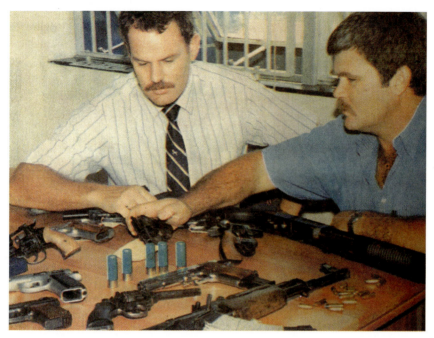

Johan, a captain at the time, and Sergeant Ian Fitchat with an arms cache recovered from a cash-in-transit robbery in 1991. Fitchat was shot and killed on duty a few years later. (*The Daily News*, edited by Gerhard de Bruin)

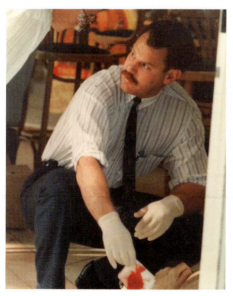

Johan at a crime scene in Durban in 1992. (SAPS file)

Johan (far right) bending over a dead suspect at the Essenwood Road shooting in Durban on 20 July 1993. (SAPS file)

Because of their safety features, Mercedes-Benz cars were frequently used to ram cash-in-transit vehicles. (SAPS file)

Johan with Lieutenant Colonel Zethembe Chonco. (*The Daily News*)

Crime scene: Lieutenant Colonel Zethembe Chonco's assassination on 27 August 2008. (Mossie Mostert)

One of Chonco's assassins was killed in a return of fire on 27 August 2008. (Mossie Mostert)

Johan shortly after landing on the N3 freeway on 16 September 2008. Newspaper reports and the state would later accuse him of having planted an AK-47 at the crime scene. (Ian Carbutt/ *The Witness*)

Johan (far left) and Provincial Commissioner Hamilton Ngidi at the crime scene of Inkosi Mbongeleni Zondi's murder on 22 January 2009. At least 50 cartridges were found at the scene. (SAPS file)

Johan in 2011 on a police patrol boat en route to the Greek vessel *Irene* as part of an Interpol anti-piracy operation. (SAPS file)

Approaching the *Irene* in a rubber duck. Johan is front left in a HAWKS cap, with Willie Olivier directly behind him and Antonio Montanaro, from Interpol, right of Johan. (SAPS file)

Provincial Commissioner Mmamonnye Ngobeni in Durban after an anti-crime beach walk. Johan is on the far left. (Anil Singh/Media24)

Accused number 1, Johan, comes up into court from the holding cells on 21 February 2016 after being recharged. (Thuli Dlamini/Times Media)

In court: Accused number 1, Johan, is on the far left and Willie Olivier on the far right. (Personal collection)

Johan in discussion with investigating officer Colonel Pharasa Ncube (left) and Willie Olivier (right). (Thuli Dlamini/Times Media)

Johan in court with Willie Olivier (left) and attorney Carl van der Merwe (right). (Personal collection)

National Police Commissioner Riah Phiyega (left) speaks at a press conference in Durban, on 7 February 2014, as Provincial Commissioner Mmamonnye Ngobeni looks on. (Giordano Stolley/Allied Picture Press)

The National Director of Public Prosecutions, Advocate Shaun Abrahams (left) and Deputy National Director of Public Prosecutions Nomgcobo Jiba (right) at the NPA's head office in Pretoria on 7 July 2015. (Reinart Toerien/EWN)

The head of the Hawks, Lieutenant General Berning Ntlemeza. (Giordano Stolley/Allied Picture Press)

Johan with Major General Alfred Khana, who was sent to get a warning statement from him on 31 March 2016. (Personal collection)

Johan with former Springbok fullback André Joubert, who donated his 1995 Rugby World Cup blazer to raise funds for Cato Manor court challenges. (Personal collection)

A Booysen family wedding in Rome in 2013. From left: Morné, Melissa, Natalie, André, Letithia, Johan, Liza and Eben. (Personal collection)

call from the National Police Commissioner, who had heard about the investigation from Dramat.

Bheki Cele instructed me to take charge of the investigation and not to entertain interference. I knew that he and General Ngobeni had once been very close; I wasn't sure what had prompted this. There must have been other dynamics at play.

Cele told Johan that independent forensic auditors would be appointed. Johan wrote to finance, instructing them to freeze the payout of Panday's remaining money, a further R15 million.

One night a month or so later Ngobeni phoned just as Johan was having dinner at a restaurant on Durban's Bluff. She was agitated. She told Johan she had heard that Panday was making a statement against her. Did he know anything about it? He didn't, but reckoned Panday, via Madhoe, was threatening to expose the donation to her husband's birthday party, unless the investigation was stopped and his R15 million was released by the SAPS finance department.

Johan told her to calm down and assured her that Panday had made no such statement. She kept repeating: 'Are you sure? Are you sure?'

For a supposedly innocent person, he thought she sounded very guilty.

Encouraged by Bheki Cele's go-ahead, Johan told the Hawks to obtain search warrants for Panday's house, business premises and vehicles. And, in an unprecedented move, warrants for SAPS HQ itself. They would need specific documents from Supply Chain Management as well as Madhoe's laptop. For this Johan's team recruited Hawks commercial crime experts from Pietermaritzburg and Port Shepstone to make sure the warrant was executed correctly. It could not be a fishing expedition.

I was apprehensive about searching HQ without the PC's knowledge. I visualised her reaction when officers ultimately under her command burst in and began searching her building. I had to be tactical.

He told the men to assemble at 6am on the same morning that he and General Ngobeni were due to attend a parliamentary Lekgotla in Umbilo. As they walked into the Lekgotla at 9am, he took a pre-arranged phone call then informed her that HQ was being searched.

There was nothing she could do. She was about to report back to the KZN parliament about the state of crime in the province. She was trapped.

But by the time the investigators got to Panday's house, he wasn't there – they suspected he'd been alerted. When they phoned him, he said he was in Newcastle, three hours away. They informed him they would spend the day at his house if necessary. He was there within the hour. Incriminating documents were seized.

During the raids a copy of Johan's report was found in Madhoe's car.

When Johan later asked Ngobeni how this confidential document could've ended up with Madhoe, suspecting that she'd given Madhoe her copy, she brushed him aside: 'Anyone could've given it to him.'

According to an affidavit by Cato Manor detective Mossie Mostert, Panday approached him a few weeks later offering to pay him to destroy evidence. At first Mostert didn't know who he was: 'I got this phone call from a guy saying he needed to tell me something. I thought he had information. I arranged to meet him at a garage. When I got there I realised I'd met him before through a colleague. He said he needed my help and explained that he'd been accused of fraud.'

Panday, said Mostert, wanted him to steal the documents seized from his office. He told him exactly where they were being stored, a supposedly secret location, as well as the file numbers. If he couldn't get his hands on them, Panday said, he should set the building alight. Mostert refused: 'I said I couldn't do that and he said: "Name your price." I suspected it was a setup and I phoned General Booysen.'

Johan was at a conference in Johannesburg. He rushed home, berated Mostert for not keeping Panday hanging on and told him to call Panday and say he'd changed his mind. They applied for a 252 authority, which would allow Crime Intelligence to rig Mostert's car with a recorder and cameras. But at the meeting Mostert set up soon after, he says Panday smelt a rat and wouldn't go near the car.

At the end of 2010, Panday took SAPS to court to have the subpoenas overturned, but his application was eventually dismissed with costs.

Panday failed to get the Section 205s set aside, he failed to get Ngobeni to stop the investigation and he failed to get Mostert to destroy evidence. But it would be Panday's final attempt to save himself that Johan found the most extraordinary of all.

As far as I was concerned I had an unblemished 38-year career in the police. I was against corruption. I found it incredible that they thought they could bribe me.

- 10 -
'(2)' IN THE BOOT

The Panday procurement investigation continued in 2011, and after a lengthy tender procedure, PricewaterhouseCoopers was appointed to do a money-trail analysis.

Johan spent part of the first half of 2011 working with Interpol on a piracy investigation off the African coast. It involved a supertanker called *Irene SL*, which was pirated off the coast of Oman in February. After two months the ransom was paid – a record amount of $13.5 million – and the tanker moved just off the port of Durban, where Johan and a team of South African forensic investigators assisted French, German and Italian police in processing the vessel as a crime scene.

Back in the office in August, Sergeant Deena Govender, one of the Hawks, approached him and told him that Navin Madhoe wanted to talk. Johan assumed it must be about Panday and the ongoing investigation. Govender said Madhoe wanted to meet at the Jaipur Palace restaurant in Durban North. But in case it was a setup, Johan changed the venue to the Elangeni Hotel, not far from SAPS HQ.

Madhoe, accompanied by Deena, arrived shortly after me. He had on a leather jacket and tie and had a laptop, which he opened. He showed me photographs, mostly of dead bodies. Some I recognised because I'd been at the scene, some I didn't. So what, I thought. Madhoe pushed papers around all day and had probably never even been to a crime scene.

Madhoe snapped the laptop shut and said he could get more pictures. He asked Govender to leave so he could speak to Johan privately. He wanted to talk about the investigation against him and 'TP', as he called Panday. Johan told him the investigation wasn't going anywhere.

It wasn't true, but it soon became pretty clear to me where he was going. He thought the photographs were linked to me and wanted to bribe me. In return for the pictures, he said, I should pre-date the report about him and Panday – the same report we'd seized from his car. It hadn't been dated or stamped.

Aware that evidence obtained without a Section 205 could be inadmissible in court, Madhoe wanted Johan to antedate the report so that it looked like the bank records had been illegally obtained – that is before the Section 205 was issued. It would become fruit of the poisonous tree and get thrown out in court.

In return, Madhoe said, he would give him the rest of the photographs. He gave Johan a memory stick of the pictures he'd just shown him.

I knew I couldn't engage Madhoe any further without a Section 252, which allows evidence obtained in a trap to be admissible in a criminal trial. I left the meeting and made arrangements to obtain a 252 from the deputy director of public prosecutions for the go-ahead to engage Madhoe.

The next afternoon Madhoe phoned and told Johan to meet him in his car in the parking bay downstairs. As soon as Johan arrived Madhoe asked if he'd brought the report. Johan told him he couldn't find it.

He reached over to the back seat, retrieved an envelope and pulled out the self-same document and said: 'Pre-date this one.'

Johan had made only two copies; he suspected that Ngobeni must have given hers to Madhoe.

The game was on. I decided to play along and see what was on offer. He didn't mention the photographs again, but it was clear to me that he regarded them as his trump card.

Johan sent the document to forensics to be examined for fingerprints and DNA. Panday's fingerprints were found on it.

Four days later, on 31 August 2011, he met with Madhoe again. He gave Johan a hard drive saying 'everything had been erased'. Realising that Madhoe now wanted the antedated document, Johan told him everything came at a price. This was obviously what Madhoe had been waiting for. Johan says Madhoe's eyes lit up:

He said: I'll let the bastard [Panday] pay for what he put me through and then asked me how much.

Johan said he would send him a figure and that Madhoe should add three zeros.

Johan waited five days, during which time he went to Pretoria to brief his boss, Anwa Dramat. He showed Dramat a text message he'd received from Madhoe after they met:

Good morning Gen. wot happened no sms. when u back. (2)

Dramat and Johan assumed the '(2)' meant R20 000.

On his return to Durban, he met Madhoe at McDonald's at Gateway Shopping Centre, where Johan was told 'TP' had got together 'one bar'. Another bar would be forthcoming.

The '(2)' had meant R2 million. Johan was astonished.

They were obviously very worried about the investigation and what had been uncovered.

Madhoe asked if he should do a bank transfer to the account of a friend or family member. They agreed on cash: R1.5 million in R200 notes, the balance on delivery of the signed and dated document.

The following day, 7 September, was RC Maharaj's funeral. The Cato Manor officer had been killed near Chatsworth. He'd been investigating a murder when he was shot through a door and was hit in the chest just above his bulletproof vest. He died in hospital. Bheki Cele spoke at the funeral. Johan knew RC's family well.

His mother Auntie Lallipore was deeply affected – she worshipped RC. His death affected everyone.

Madhoe was at the funeral and sidled up to Johan. He told him he couldn't get R200 notes from the bank and that the cash would fit into three boxes – the kind that reams of A4 paper came in. He said the date on the document had to be 10 May 2010 – before the 205s had been obtained from the court.

'(2)' IN THE BOOT

Madhoe wrote 10 May 2010 on an ATM slip. Useful evidence that there'd been contact, thought Johan as he took it.

We arranged for the handover to take place the following day at 9.00am.

That evening Crime Intelligence told Johan there'd been contact between Madhoe and a policeman called Sandesh Dhaniram.

'The *gora* ["white man"] is eating out of my hand,' Madhoe had told Dhaniram.

Dhaniram had once worked at Organised Crime, directly under Colonel Aiyer, the unit commander. He said in a statement written in September 2011 that earlier that year Aiyer had given him a CD of crime scene photographs downloaded from a Cato Manor computer and told him to identify the bodies, find the families and go and interview them. But then Dhaniram was transferred. His new position took him to HQ on occasion, where he came into contact with Madhoe, says Johan.

Everyone knew that Madhoe was, thanks to me, the subject of an internal procurement investigation. According to Crime Intelligence, Dhaniram told Madhoe that Aiyer had given him a CD of photographs that could be used to compromise me. Madhoe was very interested, so Dhaniram gave him the disc.

All of this Johan pieced together much later, after Dhaniram made his statement. But it was those same photographs that were being used to try to blackmail him.

Once he'd handed them over, Dhaniram told Madhoe he was worried he'd be implicated. Madhoe assured him that 'his man' Thoshan would protect him.

•

On 8 September, Ngobeni was away on official business in Pretoria and Johan was standing in as acting provincial commissioner. He felt overwhelmed. In addition to heading up provincial police, he was also trying to juggle a covert investigation.

Elaine, my PA, looked at me strangely as I rushed in and out of the office without telling her where I was going. Normally I fill her in on my movements.

He had organised for Colonel Len Sheriff from the Hawks to help him with the document handover to Madhoe. Johan wanted to meet at the Sun Coast Casino because there were cameras there. Madhoe favoured the Hyper by the Sea in Durban North. Eventually they agreed on the basement parking at SAPS HQ.

The last thing Johan wanted was for Madhoe to get away with his report, which he had now signed and antedated.

It was agreed that Colonel Sheriff and other Hawks officers would be positioned across the road and on the fire escape and would pounce as I gave a signal: I would touch my head.

As Johan got out of the lift in the basement, armed with a spy camera, he saw Madhoe.

It seemed like he wanted to do the handover right there. But it was out of the view of the waiting officers, so I told him to rather reverse his car next to mine.

He reversed, opened his boot, took out a brand-new suitcase and put it into Johan's boot. Johan asked to see inside. Madhoe opened the suitcase. It was packed with R100 and R50 notes.

My timing had to be perfect – after the boot shut on the moneybag, but before he got into his car. My mouth was dry, my heart was beating. I had never partaken in something like this – I felt uncomfortable.

Johan handed over the document and touched his head. Nothing happened. Madhoe got into his car. Johan touched his head again. The officers on the fire escape pounced before Madhoe had travelled 20 metres.

Johan didn't look at him.

I went back upstairs and someone asked me what was wrong. Clearly I looked unsettled. Then I went back and handed my car keys to Colonel Sheriff so they could count the money and do forensics on the vehicle.

Back in his office he looked at the spycam footage: it was all there.

I sent Ngobeni a text message, telling her that Madhoe had been arrested for attempted bribery. It must have spoiled her day.

The following day Sheriff came to his office to tell him he'd been short-changed. There was just under R1.4 million in the bag. Johan laughed – Panday had had the temerity to attempt to bribe him and then short-changed him.

Back in the cells at Durban Central, Madhoe made a full confession to Sheriff, implicating himself and Thoshan Panday. Panday was arrested at the airport on 24 September 2011, on his return from a trip to the Democratic Republic of Congo. He was charged with fraud and corruption.

He said in an affidavit: 'This arrest, I verily believe, happened because of my refusal to implicate the KZN Provincial Commissioner.'

Panday was in custody for two weeks before being released on R100 000 bail in October 2011. While in prison Johan says Panday allegedly approached a Mozambican man called Pinto – who later supplied Johan with an affidavit – asking him if he could organise a hitman to take Johan out.

As payment for killing me, he said Panday had promised him South African citizenship.

In custody Madhoe had time to think and talk to his attorney, who told him not to implicate himself or Panday. It was then, says Johan, that Madhoe changed his tune.

Without batting an eyelid, he changed his account. He said it was me who had wanted to buy the photographs from him and that I had given him the bag of money, not the other way round.

Johan was to pay the balance on receipt of material implicating officers from the Cato Manor unit in unlawful activities. But, Madhoe said, when he took the money to his 'contacts' they had refused to accept the lesser amount. When he was arrested, he wrote in an affidavit, he was actually returning the money to Booysen.

Johan couldn't believe Madhoe thought he'd get away with such barefaced lies.

Why would I want to buy non-incriminating photographs? I could have got them off our database. But I wasn't concerned – there was more evidence against them.

Besides the confession, investigators had found a slip in the cash Madhoe had given him. It was traced to a bank withdrawal made by Panday's brother's girlfriend's father, proving that it wasn't Johan's money. After being approached by the investigators, the father made a statement, saying he had withdrawn the money. Panday's fingerprints were on the report Madhoe had given Johan to be signed; there was spycam footage of the money being handed over and it had been witnessed by at least two Hawks officers. There were also cellphone intercepts that implicated the two of them and showed exactly where they were when they had made the calls.

Panday's advocate, Jimmy Howse, said at his bail application that his client thought it was absurd for anyone to believe that he would part with millions for 'such a risky deal'.

Unbeknown to Johan, and in a move that linked Panday to a much wider network, suspended Crime Intelligence head Lieutenant General Richard Mdluli drove to KZN from Gauteng to speak with Colonel Subramoney, whom Johan had originally appointed to investigate Panday. At a meeting in Ballito, Mdluli told Subramoney his life was in grave danger. He should transfer to Johannesburg as a matter of urgency and continue working on the Panday investigation from there.

Subramoney was told to tell everyone at Durban HQ he had resigned.

Johan was surprised when he heard and questioned the decision.

He told me he was fed up and needed to do something else with his life. I tried to persuade him to stay and told him he shouldn't give up after a few punches on the chin. A few months later I heard rumours that he'd joined Crime Intelligence.

But in July 2014, Subramoney would testify that he had been lured away from Durban by Mdluli and dumped in an office in Benoni. There, his attempts to continue the Panday investigation had been thwarted. He said his life had become a living hell; he was never allocated any work and had lost all sense of self-worth, attempting suicide more than once. His passion for his work had diminished and his life been rendered useless, he said, because of his attempts to uncover corruption.

Johan, unaware of the reason for Subramoney's departure at the time, had no idea that Panday had such influence. That is until the day his PA Elaine told him the president's brother was looking for him. He'd phoned several times, she said. Johan was sure it wasn't the president's brother, but told Elaine to tell whomever it was to make an appointment to come to his office if he wanted to see him. Life and work intervened, but a few months later, President Zuma's son, Edward, arrived. He and Johan sat in his office making small talk – until Edward came out with it.

He said he had invested R900 000 in one of Panday's businesses and wasn't getting his dividends because Panday said I had frozen his payments. He asked whether I could release Panday's R15 million. I told him that I couldn't do that or I'd be guilty of corruption myself.

Then Johan gave him some advice.

'(2)' IN THE BOOT

I told him to demand his R900 000 back from Thoshan Panday. Once he had it he should take it and run and not look back. Months later, a friend phoned me and said someone was with him and wanted to talk to me. It was Edward. I jokingly asked if he had taken my advice. He said he had. I didn't believe him.

- 11 -
THE FIFTH COLUMN

'Sadly, in many respects, the Fourth Estate has become the fifth column of democracy, colluding with the powers that be in a culture of deception that subverts the thing most necessary to freedom, and that is the truth.'
– Bill Moyers, US journalist and commentator in a 2008 article 'Is the Fourth Estate a Fifth Column' published in *In These Times*, a monthly magazine by the Institute for Public Affairs in Chicago

Sunday 11 December 2011. The COP17 climate change conference was underway in Durban – using too many police resources, Johan thought. He walked down the steep hill to his front gate to get his newspapers. He planned to glance at them over a cup of coffee before getting ready for church, where he conducted the choir.

He unfolded the *Sunday Times* on his kitchen counter while he waited for the kettle to boil.

He did a double take.

INSIDE A SOUTH AFRICAN POLICE 'DEATH SQUAD'
Today the Sunday Times lifts the lid on killings committed by an elite police unit.

Special investigation by Stephan Hofstatter, Mzilikazi Wa Afrika and Rob Rose

On the front page there was a photograph of 11 men having a party.

'Shoot to Kill ... and have a beer with your mates afterwards.'

Johan recognised the men in the photos, even though faces had been blurred. Most of them were from the Cato Manor Unit. Raymond Lee with his shirt off, his hand on his holster; Eugene van Tonder holding his gun aloft; Shane Naidoo pointing his at the camera. Mossie Mostert's head peered out from behind Anton Lockem's outstretched arm. There were booze bottles everywhere – Black Label and Captain Morgan.

Johan recalled the occasion. The photograph had been taken on 21 January 2009. Although unrelated, it had been the day before the murder of Inkosi Zondi.

It had started as a lunchtime braai at the Cato Manor office. I was invited, but before the coals were ready the guys were called out to a robbery. I left to go to choir practice.

The *Sunday Times* called it a 'post-kill' party: 'Members of the Cato Manor Organised Crime Unit celebrate just hours after killing five robbery suspects on the N3 highway near Camperdown,' read the caption.

At the time, News24 had reported the incident somewhat differently:

5 ROBBERS KILLED IN SHOOTOUT
21 JANUARY 2009

Johannesburg – KwaZulu-Natal police shot dead five suspected robbers and arrested four others in Camperdown on Wednesday.

Superintendent Henry Budhram said police received a tip-off about nine armed men on a minibus taxi on their way to Pietermaritzburg, allegedly to commit a robbery.

Police followed the vehicle and stopped it before the Lion Park turn-off on the N3.

The suspects alighted and fired shots at the police who returned fire.

The *Sunday Times* said the victims had been shot in the head at close range, indicating that they hadn't been fleeing. It didn't mention the four who had been arrested.

The series of articles – and the accompanying captioned images – were intended to evoke images of the apartheid-era police hit squads – and certainly did. The main story even quoted an SACP provincial leader as saying that the Cato Manor squad was 'the new Vlakplaas'.

On an inside page was a photograph that Johan also recognised. It was an incident that had occurred not more than a week later, but hadn't directly involved Cato Manor – even if it ran with the caption: 'The bloody trail of the killer cops: unidentified bodies, allegedly killed by police "hit squads" in KZN in January 2009.' It was a photograph of five dead men on the back of a bakkie.

Johan had been at the Durban harbour with a team of detectives from Pietermaritzburg on that day, impounding cocaine on a Russian ship.

While I was there, a butchery that also served as a pension payout had been robbed. There had been a car chase and a shoot-out involving the Flying Squad and the K9 Unit. It had ended with the robbers being killed. After I had finished at the harbour, I went to the scene, at Maydon Wharf.

Eight robbers were dead and three members of the public were injured, one of them a motorist, who was shot in the chest when a bullet went through his windscreen.

Members of the K9 dog Unit had shot the robbers. Cato Manor was called in to do the robbery investigation. But now, almost three years later, the *Sunday Times* implied that the same 'death squad' they had shown partying on the front page had killed the men shown lying in the bakkie.

While doing the investigation, Cato Manor detective Shane Naidoo had obtained the photos of the dead men from the Criminal Record Centre and loaded them onto the office computer to see if they could be linked to other crimes; he would find out later they were linked to two other armed robbers and had been travelling in a hijacked car.

But the *Sunday Times* said the photograph had been 'circulating' among top cops in recent weeks, providing incriminating evidence of assassinations. Below the picture of the dead suspects was a list of what the *Sunday Times* called 'blood-curdling cases' between 2008 and 2009. 'Killings', they wrote, 'which often took place in broad daylight, all committed by this elite KwaZulu-Natal unit based in Cato Manor.'

Some of the dead suspects listed were connected to Chonco's murder; others were alleged robbers, murderers and ATM bombers.

In all of these cases, seasoned senior policemen, as well as ballistics and pathology experts – speaking to the *Sunday Times* on strict condition of anonymity – raise serious doubts about the official versions of events. While the ICD was established to probe these kinds of alleged police abuses, question marks hang over whether it has the capacity or will to do any serious investigation.

On page five there was a picture of two Cato Manor Unit policemen in plain clothes, Bruce McInnes and the late RC Maharaj, arms raised in celebration – or perhaps just fooling around for the camera. To the left of them was warrant officer, Asogram Pillay, smiling, his feet up and arms folded. Next to him a woman has her shirt to her nose and mouth. She could be crying; she could be sneezing; she could be wiping her nose.

The *Sunday Times* went with an image headline: 'The Death Squads Who Kill with a Grin' and captioned it with: 'Ghoulish Glee: Members of the Cato Manor organised crime unit in a good mood after shooting two suspects at a homestead in KwaZulu-Natal in 2008, while someone, who appears to be a family member of the deceased, weeps.'

What the *Sunday Times* didn't tell their readers was that the photograph was taken at 6:22am, three hours after the shooting of the two suspects near Melmoth, 200 kilometres north of Durban. The policemen in the photograph had been on duty for almost 24 hours and were waiting for a SAPS duty officer to arrive to process the scene.

Johan recognised some of the photographs in the spread as those that Madhoe had shown him at the Elangeni and tried to blackmail him with – the same images Dhaniram said he had got from Aiyer on a CD.

But in the Sunday Times *Madhoe came across as a hero, as someone who had tried to blow the whistle on this alleged police hit squad operating in KZN.*

Booysen, Madhoe told the newspaper, had requested a meeting with him and had asked for the images because they contained 'incriminating evidence of serious crimes in a unit under his direct command'. He told the *Sunday Times* that his action was 'duly recorded' and that 'certain select police officers and intelligence were well aware of it'.

Johan thought it outrageous that Madhoe was being made out to be a super sleuth.

I regarded him as a glorified purchasing clerk, who couldn't have conducted a covert operation if he tried. Furthermore, he would have needed permission from provincial prosecutors by obtaining 252 authority. He hadn't done that. I had, in order to investigate him and Panday.

There was even a sidebar devoted to Johan. Mention was made of the fact that he joined the police in 1976, the year of the Soweto uprising.

WHO IS JOHAN BOOYSEN?

It has taken Major General Johan Booysen 35 years to rise to his position as head of the Hawks in KwaZulu-Natal. He joined the police in 1976 – the year in which the Soweto riots drew attention to the atrocities committed by the South African Police.

Johan would much later complain to the press ombudsman:

Their ... subliminal reporting is designed to garner public support and to elicit emotions ... they refer to me as having joined the police during the Soweto youth riots. This is irrelevant ... I was an innocent youth myself when I joined the police.

The *Sunday Times* also quoted from an interview it had done with Johan.

'He denied that this unit under his control conducted a series of "hits" in revenge for cop killings, and urged witnesses to come forward. "That's why we have legal processes," he said. "Let's allow these cases to be investigated by the ICD and presented to the prosecuting authority."

'But the witnesses who spoke to the *Sunday Times* said they were petrified of coming forward, lest they too end up being taken out on a quiet road while "resisting arrest".'

Johan doubted there were ever witnesses and challenged the *Sunday Times* in a letter to the ombudsman.

The newspaper responded that the witnesses it had interviewed had refused to cooperate with authorities, fearing for their lives: 'Booysen's claim that we have fabricated these witnesses is insulting.'

The newspaper said that several of its sources had 'been killed or died in strange circumstances'.

Johan challenged them to reveal these sources.

Surely they cannot be killed again?

•

Johan had been tipped off about the article a few weeks before it was published.

Major General Deena Moodley, the head of Crime Intelligence in KZN, had told me that he'd met with two Sunday Times *journalists in Pietermaritzburg. Also present at the meeting between investigative journalists Stephan Hofstatter and Mzilikazi Wa Afrika was a policeman friend of Panday's.*

General Moodley had told Johan that the *Sunday Times* was going to run a story implicating him and planned to phone him on the Saturday before publication that Sunday.

Johan got his lawyer, Carl van der Merwe, to contact the *Sunday Times*, saying he was aware of the impending story and would like to respond in a reasonable time period.

The following week Stephan Hofstatter came to see me. I had met him before – he had once interviewed me about Ngobeni's involvement in a multimillion-rand building lease.

Sitting in Johan's office, Hofstatter phoned Wa Afrika and put him on speakerphone. They asked Johan about the shooting of Magojela Ndimande and Tembe on the N3 three years before, which the article would describe as having occurred with:

'No lights, no warnings, just a barrage of rifle fire, and a taxi boss and his bodyguard were dead – at the hands of rogue cops ...'

In his office Hofstatter asked for Johan's response to allegations that he'd arrived on the scene in a helicopter soon afterwards and congratulated Organised Crime officers.

I told them they could verify my arrival time with the SAPS Air Wing. It would be in the pilot's logbook – I had landed 90 minutes after the shooting. As investigative journalists, I imagined they'd follow this up. I didn't know it then but I would later be accused by the state of 'tampering with the crime scene and placing an AK-47 rifle ... to create an impression that the deceased was armed ...' Obviously this was the scenario the Sunday Times *was trying to fabricate as well.*

In the article, the journalists wrote about the incident: 'Ndimande and Tembe now dead, the police calmly put on their police jackets and, a few seconds later, a convoy of marked police vans arrived. Minutes later Booysen himself landed in a police chopper.'

The newspaper also included a photograph of Johan greeting Colonel Hennie Laatz, from Organised Crime, on the scene in Pietermaritzburg. Behind them is an SUV, doors open and a body on the ground. The caption reads: 'Major General Johan Booysen ... arrived by police helicopter at the scene of one of the killings.' The accompanying article says: 'The image of Booysen landing victoriously on the scene was plastered all over newspapers the next day ...'

What does 'landing victoriously' mean? The pilot landed in the middle of the highway because that's where we needed to be. I shook Colonel Laatz's hand because that's what I do when I meet someone. As provincial commander I regularly attended scenes by helicopter.

Johan started making inquiries as to the source of the information and why the *Sunday Times* was trying to create the impression that his arrival at the scene had been carefully synchronised. In his view, all roads led to Panday.

Crime Intelligence told me that Wa Afrika and Thoshan Panday had been communicating. Wa Afrika had told Panday that there was 'solid rock' evidence against me. The arrest of 'Mr B' was imminent, that he could guarantee.

Then, according to the source, the conversation had shifted. Wa Afrika told Panday he needed to find the Magojela Ndimande docket – 'File 106 9 2008 Howick'. It would reveal how Booysen had blocked Ndimande's car with his chopper, after which 'others came and killed him'.

Panday had followed up and phoned a contact at the Mountain Rise Police Station in Pietermaritzburg and asked him to get hold of the file. But he was told the docket was with the ICD.

Johan's source told him that Wa Afrika had arranged to meet Panday at the Gateway Shopping Centre in Umhlanga.

There, Panday would give him a CD of damning evidence against Booysen and Cato Manor. The CD from Colonel Rajen Aiyer would be the smoking gun.

But as the time for the handover grew closer, the CD wasn't forthcoming. Johan knew there was no such CD.

But there did seem to be a very well-orchestrated campaign against me. Why was a journalist involved in trying to discredit a senior police official and in the process abetting a suspect in a multimillion-rand corruption investigation? It was unethical, if not criminal. I thought it had something to do with attempts to oust National Police Commissioner Bheki Cele.

The *Sunday Times* story had made a point of linking Johan and Cele: 'Booysen is at pains to deny reports of a close relationship with suspended police chief Bheki Cele, saying he barely knew the man and had been at the police chief's house only once – and that was on official business. Booysen said Cele played no part in his promotion, even though he would have had to approve the appointment.'

They had also been linked in Richard Mdluli's Ground Coverage Intelligence Report, which had alleged: 'General Booysen was given the post at the DPCI to protect [Bheki] Cele's interests and also that he is the current day Vlakplaas commander and knows of the skeletons in Cele's closet.' It made Johan wonder who else, other than Panday, Hofstatter and Wa Afrika had talked to.

The author of the Ground Coverage Report had been Crime Intelligence officer NH Singh. Before the release of the report he had been transferred from Durban to Pretoria to work directly under Mdluli, where the discredited report was allegedly concocted.

Years later, in a series of letters written between the *Sunday Times*, Johan and the press ombudsman, the *Sunday Times* admitted to the press ombudsman that NH Singh had been a source for the Cato Manor story. To date no hearing has taken place because Johan was recharged by the NPA.

While many felt the newspaper had been used to settle scores, Hofstatter and Wa Afrika went on to win several journalism awards for the 'Death Squad' stories.

They had also won an award for a story that resulted in Bheki Cele's axing as National Police Commissioner. It was called 'Police Commissioner General Bheki Cele and the SAPS building lease'.

Back in August 2010, Wa Afrika had exposed a fishy R500-million lease agreement for new police headquarters in Pretoria. The police chief, it was reported, had signed the deal to move SAPS HQ to a building owned by a businessman, Roux Shabangu, without following tender procedures.

Cele had held a news conference two days later and called Wa Afrika 'a very shady journalist', and the next day Gauteng Hawks General Shadrack Sibiya had arrested Wa Afrika outside the *Sunday Times* offices. He was handcuffed, his house searched and he was imprisoned overnight on charges of fraud and forgery. There was an outcry.

Wa Afrika sued SAPS for wrongful arrest and the state settled out of court. Johan remembers at the time thinking how unnecessary it was.

I had reservations about the arrest. Why not send him a summons or arrange with his lawyers for him to report to court? I didn't realise it would have wider implications.

In September, Shadrack Sibiya would lead the investigation into Crime Intelligence chief Richard Mdluli, which resulted in the latter's arrest for the murder of Oupa Ramogibe, who was married to Mdluli's former girlfriend.

Just weeks later, the *Sunday Times* reported that Sibiya and national Hawks head Anwa Dramat were involved in illegally repatriating Zimbabweans wanted for crimes back home: 'Senior officials in the Hawks and SA Police Service are conducting illegal "renditions" with their Zimbabwean counterparts – by arresting "suspects" and illegally sending them across the Beit Bridge border to be murdered.'

The *Sunday Times* denied that Mdluli's crony and Crime Intelligence CFO Solly Lazarus had planted the article to cast suspicion on the investigating team. But in a report, the Hawks' Kobus Roelofse said that a Crime Intelligence officer had overheard a discussion at Lazarus' house.

> On 10 October 2011 ... he heard them discussing the placement of a newspaper article relating to Lieutenant General Dramat and Major General Sibiya. He stated that Major General Lazarus wanted to use sources within the media (journalists paid by CI) to write a story in order to take the focus away from them. This,

according to the member, is a strategy employed to cast suspicion on those they perceive to be a threat.

Johan would later come to feel as if he was being dragged into a storm of seemingly unrelated events and created by those wanting to get rid of Bheki Cele and to promote Richard Mdluli.

The *Sunday Times* has maintained that its stories on Booysen and Cato Manor were not the result of a plant by Crime Intelligence. It had, the newspaper said, been alerted to 'an unusually high number of suspicious killings', involving Cato Manor, as well as to threats made to taxi operators in KwaZulu-Natal.

•

On the Monday after the *Sunday Times* death squad story, Johan went to work, naively thinking it would all blow over. But it didn't.

Instead, Hawks head Anwa Dramat appointed a team to investigate the Cato Manor squad under the leadership of three major generals – Jan Mabula, Yvonne Badi and Liziwe Ntshinga.

While Johan waited to see what their first move would be, he got busy with thwarting Thoshan Panday's efforts to get his R15 million unfrozen.

I told his lawyers I'd release it if Panday could prove the money was owed to him.

Panday set about trying to do that, without Madhoe, who had been suspended after his arrest in August 2011. Panday turned to his other alleged police contacts, Aswin Narainpershad and Kevin Stephen, whom the Hawks suspected were working with Panday.

Johan saw Stephen in the lift one day in January 2012 and gave him the eye, subtly letting him know he knew about his Panday connection.

Stephen got worried and agreed to help the Hawks. After obtaining a 252 authority, we began recording his meetings with Panday. Meetings in which he offered Stephen a million rand to manufacture and generate false documents to match invoices to be submitted as claims so he could get the R15 million.

On 19 February 2012 Stephen made a statement and signed it under oath at Durban Central police station, detailing his dealings with Panday.

When he saw the spycam footage, Johan was amazed, but not surprised at the lengths Panday went to.

It was like watching a James Bond movie. They would drive round and round for 20 minutes, then go up and down the lift, hang around outside on the pavement, before finally meeting face to face. Phones would be left in their cars. Panday's manager brought a printer along and they would forge signatures before printing the documents.

Stephen said in an affidavit:

I told Thoshan I was having difficulty obtaining Brigadier Hunter's signature. He told me I must sign like Brigadier Hunter ... He then asked me to leave my phone on the table and we walked about five paces away from our cellphones ... He told me that once the documents were ready he would give me something ... he would give me One Bar. I accepted and said that the deal was done. I then left and phoned Colonel Sheriff ... I handed the shirt with the recording device to him.

Five days later, on 25 January 2012:

While driving, Thoshan kept looking in his rear view mirrors; he appeared to be very nervous. I told him I had the stuff and opened my briefcase. I showed him the signed documents. I told him I had forged Brigadier Hunter's signature. Thoshan showed me a thumbs-up. I showed him the invoices that I had signed and backdated and certified as services rendered. He said that I did a good job. I told him I would leave my briefcase with him and he said no, he cannot be seen with the documents ...

At one of their meetings, Panday told Stephen that the case against Madhoe was going to be dropped. Stephen wrote that Thoshan further stated that '"they" interviewed him and wanted to give him an affidavit [*sic*] about Booysen and what was in the photos, how many CDs ... and not to worry because "we" are working on that. He did not say who they or we were.'

'They' must have been Jan Mabula and the team investigating Cato Manor, Johan thought.

So much for impartiality. Panday, the suspect, was being consulted and not only for evidence against me. It seemed he was in on a whole lot more.

While on the phone in Stephen's presence, Panday said to whoever was on the line: 'It is done, they will be suspended.'

Stephen recalls: 'When the call ended he turned to me and told me that General Booysen and General Moodley will be served with notices tomorrow and will be suspended.'

(Panday had accused General Moodley of illegally intercepting his communications and attempting to blackmail him.) He also told Stephen that Madhoe would be back at work on 19 January 2012, and would be placed at Durban Central police station before returning to his old job at Supply Chain Management at HQ.

Panday's predictions turned out to be true. Madhoe returned to work on that day.

And, Stephen continues: 'On 14 February 2012 I received 16 missed calls from Thoshan. When he finally got hold of me, he told me that General Booysen had received a notice of suspension.'

- 12 -

THE PLOT THICKENS

In January 2012 the man leading the investigation into Cato Manor, Major General Jan Mabula, came to see Johan. He was head of the Hawks in the North West province. And, thought Johan, he had chosen a team of investigators close to him.

He had with him Brigadier Zodwa Mokoena, said to be his girlfriend, and Colonel Tsietsi Mano, who hadn't covered himself in glory as a policeman. Mabula seemed to be ignoring Generals Badi and Ntshinga, who'd been appointed by Hawks head Anwa Dramat to investigate the allegations against me and Cato Manor.

Both Mabula and Mano had served under Richard Mdluli when he was deputy provincial commissioner in the North West. In 2008, at Mdluli's behest, they had arrested top prosecutor Gerrie Nel, then head of the Scorpions in Gauteng, in an apparent bid to prevent him acting against National Police Commissioner Jackie Selebi. Despite having insufficient evidence against Nel, Mano and Mabula had obtained an arrest warrant and 20 police officers had descended on Nel's house as if he were a wanted criminal. Nel said in a subsequent affidavit that the investigating officers had told him they were acting on orders from 'higher up'. National Prosecuting Authority (NPA) advocate Nomgcobo Jiba was suspended for having actively participated in securing the warrant for Nel's arrest.

Tsietsi Mano had a colourful history. He had been the bungling investigator in the Eugene Terre'blanche murder case. A judge had ruled most of the police evidence inadmissible because Mano had contravened the Child Justice Act. He had also once been arrested for the alleged torture of suspected bank robbers in Klerksdorp and had been sued in a civil case where a judge found that he had 'unleashed torture' on a traditional healer arrested in connection with the 2004 disappearance of police officer Frances Rasuge. The High Court found that Mano had obtained an arrest warrant for the suspect under false pretences.

Mabula also had a few skeletons in his closet, as did Brigadier Mokoena. In 2006, when Mabula was a colonel and Mokoena a captain, detectives under their command were accused of suffocating a police informer, Solomon Nengwane, to death – and getting rid of a few other suspects – while investigating a R100-million airport heist. R14 million of the recovered money had gone missing from the police safe. Mabula's men allegedly choked Nengwane with a tube. An anonymous letter sent at the time to Hawks head Anwa Dramat detailed the torture but to date IPID still hasn't concluded its investigation.

CITY PRESS
28 JULY 2013
HAWKS BOSS IN HEIST MURDER PROBE

The Independent Police Investigative Directorate (IPID) has opened a new investigation into Nengwane's death, allegedly at the hands of a task team of detectives under the command of Mabula, then a colonel, and its subsequent cover-up.

The 2006 heist, arguably the most brazen in South African history, saw about R100 million being stolen from the OR Tambo cargo terminal.

Four of the suspects in the case – inspector Khomani Mashele, civilians Tshepo Mathe, Frank Mampane and Nengwane – were killed shortly after the heist.

At the time, prosecutor Peter Smith told the court it seemed police were 'knocking off' witnesses to 'cover their own tracks'.

Johan couldn't believe that Mano, Mabula and Mokoena, with their track record, were again involved in a high-profile investigation, but he complied.

The irony was that they had been directly involved in the cover-up of a death, but had never faced the music. Yet they wanted to investigate me for incidents I wasn't involved in at all. Nonetheless, I made my office available to them – typists, fax machines, whatever they wanted. I offered them all the files pertaining to the cases.

He assumed they would be interviewing him.

I was wrong. They didn't seem the slightest bit interested in what I had to say, or what I thought were very obvious links between Aiyer, Panday and Madhoe and the Sunday Times *article.*

The first tangible sign that the investigators might have an agenda was when the investigating officer into the Inkosi Zondi murder, for which Bongani Mkhize had been a suspect, contacted Johan saying he needed to see him urgently. They arranged to meet at the KFC in Amanzimtoti. Lieutenant William Zungu had, since the Zondi investigation, been transferred to Crime Intelligence, so Johan took a recording device along in case it was a setup.

I arrived early and was fiddling with the spycam in the KFC car park when I looked up and there was Zungu. I hastily put it aside, but I suspected he'd seen it.

He needn't have worried. Zungu had come to warn him. He said someone from General Mabula's investigating team had asked him to change the statement he'd made after the death of Bongani Mkhize; they wanted him to say that Mkhize hadn't been wanted in connection with Zondi's murder, thereby implying that he'd been hunted down and killed by Cato Manor members with their own agenda.

Zungu had the distinct impression that they had wanted him to implicate Johan. He'd refused, sticking to the statement he'd made to the ICD in 2010, which was: 'During the course of my investigation information became available that ... the chairman of the KwaMaphumulo Taxi Association Bongani Mkhize was amongst those who conspired to kill Inkosi Zondi ...'

To Johan it seemed that the investigators were looking for witnesses who would prove the *Sunday Times* report, not disprove it. He felt vulnerable.

THE PLOT THICKENS

It wasn't a feeling I was accustomed to. I was used to being on top of situations. Now I wasn't sure who had what agenda and why four-year-old cases, some of which I had had nothing to do with, were being dragged up to discredit me. And why the case had been entrusted to three officers who weren't known for ethics or efficiency.

National Police Commissioner Bheki Cele had been suspended over the unlawful police leasing agreement. He and I had been lumped together in the Ground Coverage document, which was now being taken literally by the *Sunday Times*. *I suspected I was next in the firing line.*

In February 2012 Cele's temporary replacement, Lieutenant General Nhlanhla Mkhwanazi, came to see Johan. He knew him well from when Mkhwanazi had been with the Special Task Force in KZN. From being an operational cop, he was now putting out political fires. Johan had heard that Police Minister Nathi Mthethwa was pressuring him to act against Cato Manor.

Even though it was Mthethwa's connection who had alerted me to the whereabouts of Ndimande and Mkhize, I felt he was definitely in the Richard Mdluli camp, which didn't bode well for me.

Mkhwanazi told Johan that the Cato Manor detectives should become court orderlies while they waited for the investigation to be completed. Johan didn't think it appropriate at all and persuaded Mkhwanazi to instead transfer them to the narcotics section of Organised Crime.

These were top detectives. I don't want to belittle court orderlies, because they play an essential role in the criminal justice system, but the Cato Manor guys were in a different league. It seemed that the intention was to humiliate them.

An instruction came from Dramat that Cato Manor should not take on any new cases. A truck arrived, loaded up their furniture and office equipment and dumped it at their new base at Organised Crime on the seafront.

The danger to which they had exposed themselves, the nights they had spent away from home, the family time they had sacrificed and the colleagues they had lost, had ended up in what felt like shame and disgrace.

•

At HQ Johan tried to keep the relationship between himself and the provincial commissioner as polite and professional as possible, even though he didn't trust her an inch. He was confident that the case against Panday was watertight despite his connections to people in high places and that once Pricewaterhouse had finished the forensic audit, details of his dealings with Madhoe and Narainpershad at Supply Chain Management would be exposed, leading to their prosecution.

But in Pretoria, the director of the NPA's Specialised Commercial Crime Unit (SCCU), Lawrence Mrwebi, had other ideas.

Mrwebi had once led the Scorpions in KZN. His weaknesses had been so obvious that Vusi Pikoli, the former national director of public prosecutions, had described his appointment as SCCU director as 'astonishing'.[5] Pikoli had said the same about the NPA's Jiba, describing her elevation to acting national director of public prosecutions as 'baffling'. After Jiba and Mrwebi were suspended for authorising the arrest of Gerrie Nel on trumped-up charges, Richard Mdluli had submitted an affidavit in Jiba's defence.

Now the pair was back, courtesy of the president; Mrwebi as the top prosecutor in the country when it came to investigating fraud and corruption.

In December 2011 Mrwebi had withdrawn fraud charges against Mdluli. Even though there was evidence that Mdluli had misused Crime Intelligence funds, Mrwebi said the case was 'weak'. And if there was a case, he said, SAPS didn't have the right to investigate a member of Crime Intelligence – that had to be done by the Inspector General of Intelligence (IGI), which partly explained why Brigadier Simon Madonsela's investigation into the slush fund had been halted. Even though the IGI, Advocate Faith Radebe, ruled that she didn't have the powers to take over police investigations, Mrwebi insisted that Mdluli's prosecution couldn't go ahead.

'Whether there was evidence or not is in my view not important for my decision in the matter,' Mrwebi said in a memo to NPA prosecutor Glynnis Breytenbach, leaving her wondering if Mdluli was being treated differently because of who and what he knew. Breytenbach said as much to Nomgcobo Jiba and got suspended.

Perhaps encouraged by Mrwebi's way of looking at things, back in Durban, Navin Madhoe's lawyers had written to Mrwebi, requesting that he also review the investigation against their client.

It had been a Booysen and Bheki Cele plot, they said:

> Our client is adamant that the Generals have used their position to harness this unit to search, investigate, arrest, detain and harass our client to falsely implicate the KZN Provincial Commissioner General Ngobeni to ultimately protect General Cele. The alleged R60-million investigation into our client and others is a sham and a distraction to protect the true perpetrators.

Madhoe, they said, was 'a potential witness to serious crimes involving the highest echelons of the SAPS', including treason. To Johan it was an obvious attempt by Madhoe to divert attention from the charges against him.

It was so blatant, yet Mrwebi couldn't, or didn't, want to see it that way. He hadn't studied the case at all and was taking seriously the falsehoods in the letter from Madhoe's lawyers. He didn't even seem to understand why Madhoe was trying to bribe me to pre-date the report.

At the beginning of 2012 Mrwebi had written an internal memo to the Directorate of Public Prosecutions in KZN: 'How did or how could Madhoe have known about the existence of the said report? How can having it predated affect anything? Or can the report be used to prove anything?'

Booysen, he said, was a single witness in the case and the only evidence he had was 'an sms and an FNB scrap of paper'. Even though at least two Hawks investigators had seen Madhoe place the money in his car, Johan thought, and despite the slips and transactions, payments and phone calls, despite the confession and Panday's fingerprint on the document.

In his response, prosecutor Advocate Bheki Manyathi of the Durban Directorate of Public Prosecutions didn't share Mrwebi's confusion. Madhoe having had access to a confidential SAPS report was significant, he said, and he accused Mrwebi of clouding issues: 'Madhoe had a copy of the report and he knew that Booysen was the head of the Hawks who were investigating the fraud. He is making extremely serious allegations, including treason ... I fail to comprehend how the corruption matter is being used to possibly "silence" him as a potential witness.'

Why, said Manyathi, would Booysen fabricate charges against Madhoe and Panday? It wasn't because he feared the photographs – any detective could've accessed them via the SAPS database. Madhoe's allegations that Booysen had paid him for the photographs and that he'd actually been returning the money when he was arrested were, said Advocate Manyathi, 'the most absurd averment I have ever come across'.

The case against Colonel Madhoe was overwhelming, and he recommended that both Madhoe and Panday be indicted in the High Court.

•

While Madhoe was trying to wriggle off the hook, despite all the evidence against him, the probe into the Cato Manor squad had the full attention of investigators under pressure from Police Minister Mthethwa.

In February 2012, he told journalists: 'We can't have a situation where you are told there is a problem here but you've never had one single police officer facing the music and no police have been arrested to date in connection with those things.'

By then, Mthethwa had met a high-level team from the NPA, as well as the Cato Manor prosecutors. In handwritten minutes, one of the advocates present, Anthony Mosing, noted: 'Minister wants arrests in one week.'

Prosecutors were expected to knuckle down and make it happen – work through the weekend if necessary.

Johan thought it sounded highly irregular for the police minister to be reading the riot act to the NPA because the investigators were having trouble finding evidence.

Then, in a move Johan thought showed more concern about being answerable to the minister of police than to the law, Jiba phoned the prosecutions head in KZN, Simphiwe Mlotshwa, and told him to act against Cato Manor. In a sworn affidavit, Mlotshwa said she had told him:

'There is a matter where because of pressure we have to enroll as a matter of urgency.'

Mlotshwa had told Jiba to send him the supporting evidence. Instead she sent the indictment. He again asked her for the documentation to support the envisaged charges, but nothing was forthcoming.

A while later Mlotshwa was in Pretoria for a meeting and says he was called to Jiba's office. She asked why he hadn't signed the indictment. He again told her he needed the prosecution memorandum.

She must, Johan thought later, have eventually realised that she wasn't going to get Mlotshwa to dance to her tune. Instead she signed authorisations for prosecutors Sello Maema and Raymond Mathenjwa from Gauteng to act against Cato Manor in KZN.

KZN wouldn't jump, so she brought in prosecutors from elsewhere, regardless of whether there was supporting evidence or not. In my discussions with prosecutors, they said Jiba had effectively captured the independence of the DPP's office in KZN.

Later that year Mlotshwa would be removed as prosecutions head in the province and replaced by Moipone Noko, who was seen as inexperienced and regarded by Johan as more 'accommodating' than Mlotshwa was.

On 15 February 2012, SAPS served Johan with a notice of intention to suspend, exactly as Thoshan Panday had predicted to Kevin Stephen. Panday's prediction also came true for head of Crime Intelligence, General Deena Moodley, who was also suspended.

Panday accused Moodley in an affidavit of trying to 'unlawfully leverage certain concessions' from him as part of a plan to have Commissioner Ngobeni removed and replaced with Johan and of illegally bugging his phone conversations.

Panday said in an affidavit that on or about 12 September 2011 he had met Moodley at KZN police headquarters. Moodley had told him that 'he could make things very fucking bad' for him unless Panday saw things his way.

Moodley had, said Panday, played him intercepted phone calls of conversations he'd had with Edward Zuma, Madhoe and Ngobeni, expressing surprise at how familiar he was with her: 'Various conversations I had with the KwaZulu-Natal provincial commissioner were played for me. In one such conversation, I criticised her for being overweight and referred to her "big backside" and suggested that she should start losing weight.'

He had then, said Panday, called General Booysen and placed the phone on speaker: 'General Deena Moodley told General Booysen I was in his office and said further: "Is it correct that if Thoshan made an affidavit implicating the Provincial Commissioner and her husband you would play ball and not charge Thoshan and you would proceed to close CAS 781?"' General Booysen responded by saying: "Yes, it would be done immediately. We would also release his outstanding payments as well."'

Johan denies that the conversation took place.

Moodley's version was that Panday had wanted to strike a deal so that charges against him would disappear.

The *Sunday Times* had accused Moodley of bugging the conversations of journalists Hofstatter and Wa Afrika, allegedly because he'd wanted to know who'd been leaking information to them about Bheki Cele. Just for good measure, it was said he'd intercepted Cele's calls too.

Johan didn't know what to believe any more.

Moodley and I had never worked directly with each other. But because I was heading the overt investigation against Panday and he the covert operation, we were lumped together. Although I was getting my information from a different source at Crime Intelligence, the impression was that Moodley and I were in cahoots because we had crossed Panday. Then we were suspended at the same time to neutralise us.

SAPS gave Johan five days to respond to allegations that he had done nothing to stop Cato Manor from acting like a hit squad: 'You allegedly failed to act on information allegedly implicating employees under your command in serious misconduct. To wit, information of alleged unlawful or excessive use of force, and/or general unlawfulness in the shooting of one Bongani Mkhize.'

Johan wanted to know exactly what 'information' SAPS was talking about. He asked for more details so he could prepare a response. But SAPS refused his request, saying he had enough to go on. So Johan launched an urgent application in the Labour Court.

I decided to force them to treat me fairly. I wasn't going to take it lying down.

The interdict was granted: the suspension process couldn't continue until he'd received the details he sought by means of a written response.

But SAPS ignored the interdict.

Less than a month later, an officer from SAPS Human Resources came to Johan's office to tell him he'd been suspended.

My immediate commanders never once phoned me or came to suspend me. They didn't have the courage to deal with me personally. When I phoned them they wouldn't take my calls, they avoided me, which led me to believe they were acting on instructions. They invariably sent a woman to bring me the bad news – to do their dirty work. And it was always someone I didn't report to and who could never answer my questions.

The officer looked at him blankly when he asked her about the court order barring his suspension.

He went back to the Labour Court the next day. Judge David Gush ordered that his suspension be set aside and remanded contempt proceedings against SAPS and ordered them to pay his legal costs.

The following day was a public holiday – Human Rights Day 2012. It had been 52 years since Johan had watched the Harvards fly over his home in Vanderbijlpark en route to Sharpeville.

Although my suspension had been set aside and I would return to work the following day, I had a feeling that my rights were about to be trampled on.

- 13 -

THE RACKETEERS

'A relatively new charge in South African jurisprudence, racketeering is seen as a "super charge" that enables the state to convict everyone who is party to a corrupt enterprise. Introduced by the Prevention of Organised Crime Act, No. 121 of 1998, racketeering may include individuals, partnerships, corporations or any other legal entity that engages in a "pattern of racketeering activity".'
– Adriaan Basson, *Zuma Exposed*

In June 2012 Johan was about to set off on safari in northern KZN with some visiting FBI agents when he got a call that the Special Task Force was on standby to arrest the Cato Manor squad. Extra members were to be flown in from the Eastern Cape to assist with the operation.

The previous night I'd been at a farewell braai for a retiring brigadier when I heard from someone there that the team investigating Cato Manor had checked into the Blue Waters Hotel on the Durban beachfront. Now I knew why.

He asked his lawyer, Carl van der Merwe, to find out what was going on and to tell the investigators there was no need for a cloak-and-dagger operation – Cato Manor would hand themselves in if that was what was required. Van der Merwe phoned around. Jan Mabula didn't answer his phone, nor did Anwa Dramat.

Johan went on safari. On the way he heard that the arrests were imminent.

I phoned Colonel Amod Hoosen, the acting commander at Organised Crime, and told him to get all the Cato Manor guys to gather at their office. Carl should then phone General Mabula and tell him they were ready to be arrested. They needed to be as cooperative as possible. No fuss, no mess.

The Cato Manor officers waited all night, sleeping on the floor, pacing the passages. Among them was Captain Neville Eva who had been off sick for five months, suffering from organ failure.

At dawn, the homes of 18 Cato Manor officers and two officers with the National Intervention Unit (NIU) were raided. Eva's wife and their two children were woken to pounding on the door. She told reporters: 'They turned our house upside down. They removed paintings from the wall, stripped the beds, turned over couches and even went through the rubbish ...'

When they got calls from their distraught families, the men went back home. Van der Merwe's phone didn't stop: he tried to get to as many of the officers' homes as possible while the raids were underway. He phoned a dozen attorneys he knew and got them to assist individual members with the search procedure. Equipment used in the execution of their duties was being seized: computers, cellphones, cameras, firearms, blue lights and crime-scene tape.

Eighteen policemen were detained in the Durban Central police station cells, except for the two NIU members Dumisani Nzama and Sivuyile Ngodwana, who were released. They had been involved in the 2008 shooting of suspected robbers Bongani Biyela and Khanyisani Buthelezi, wanted in connection with the killing of two policemen who had been escorting a pension payout vehicle. Biyela's widow was the woman sitting next to three Cato Manor officers in the photograph the *Sunday Times* had published. The policemen had seemed in high spirits; Mrs Biyela, it was naturally assumed, was distraught.

Now, in what the NPA described as part of its 'strategy', it tried to coerce Nzama and Ngodwana into making incriminating statements against the Cato Manor members involved in the Biyela shooting.

When Cato Manor's captain Shane Smith asked if Nzama and

Ngodwana were going to be allowed access to an attorney, Smith said Brigadier Mokoena had told him to 'voertsek' (bugger off). Nzama and Ngodwana refused to change their statements. They were released that same day despite having been charged and not having appeared in court.

The Cato Manor officers spent the night in police cells.

There were celebrations at Westville Prison when prisoners heard the news. A warder later told Johan that inmates had cheered and ululated. Johan knew why.

KZN's crack police squad was out of action. They had put a lot of those guys in Westville Prison inside. It was not a popular unit among criminals. They had huge respect for Cato Manor.

The 18 accused appeared in court the following day, 21 June 2012, on 14 counts of murder, as well as housebreaking, possession of ammunition, unlawful firearms, theft, assault, pointing of firearms and malicious damage to property.

The charges dated back to an incident on 24 May 2008, with the shooting of a suspect by the name of Thabo Msimango, in Greyville. The accused officers, it was alleged, had broken open the door to Msimango's fourth-floor flat with a crowbar and shot at him as he ran to the balcony. Even though he had fallen over the edge, they were accused of continuing to fire at him as he lay on the ground. A firearm was then allegedly placed next to his body. The last charge related to the 'intentional killing' on 4 September 2011 of Qinisani Gwala, an ANC branch chairman, killed, said the state, without a warrant of arrest or tangible evidence.

THE STAR
22 JUNE 2012
CATO MANOR COPS IN COURT

It was a day of heartbreak for the family, friends and colleagues of the men who crammed into the courtroom ...

And while the State, through Advocate Raymond Mathenjwa, attempted to paint a picture that the men were simply a gang of murderous thugs, undeserving of any sympathy or of bail, the defence presented evidence of a group of hard-working policemen who worked tirelessly on 24-hour call to arrest dangerous suspects and who had co-operated fully with the six-month investigation into the 'death squad' allegations.

Led by Gauteng-based prosecutor Raymond Mathenjwa and assisted by six advocates, the state said its case was ready. Bail was opposed on the grounds that the officers posed a threat to their witnesses.

Captain Eva, testifying on behalf of those appearing, said it wasn't in their interests to harm witnesses. He also spoke about his health, which was so precarious if he picked up an infection in a dirty cell he would die, he said. (Eva died later in the year from a bacterial infection in his heart.)

Advocate Mathenjwa appeared unmoved. And callous, Johan thought, when he heard what Mathenjwa had said to Eva: 'Well, what have you done as a policeman to clean these cells that you throw others into?'

Magistrate Sharon Marx called him to order: cleaning cells wasn't the job of detectives.

Nor did Mathenjwa care that Cato Manor's Shane Naidoo had just lost his brother. He had died of a heart attack shortly after hearing the news of Shane's arrest. The court was asked by one of Naidoo's family members if he could be released to go home. Mathenjwa wasn't interested: 'Why are you telling us? Have you been informed of why he [Naidoo] is before this court? Do you know the nature of the cases against him?'

Johan, entertaining the FBI, was upset that he couldn't be at the proceedings, but showing support in the public gallery was sacked police commissioner Bheki Cele. He told reporters that the Cato Manor officers had 'repeatedly put their lives in danger to give you and I the assurance that nobody will murder you in your sleep tonight'.

CITY PRESS
23 JUNE 2012
SHOOT TO KILL IN THE DOCK

On Thursday former police chief Bheki Cele walked quietly into the courtroom to support 18 members of the Cato Manor serious and violent crimes unit who were applying for bail the day after being arrested for 14 alleged hit squad killings.

The detectives and their supporters broke into applause. Cele's a man with a well-developed sense of the theatrical.

He acknowledged them and sat directly behind his former foot soldiers, close enough to lay a hand on a shoulder. 'I may no longer be your General, but I've still got your backs,' he said.

The *Sunday Times* felt vindicated by the arrests, and carried an opinion piece by IPID's national spokesman Moses Dlamini on 1 July 2012, entitled: 'Take a Good Look at the Evidence Against "Heroes".' It was prefaced: 'Hero cops or murderers? In the past months much – both truthful and untruthful – has been written about the deadly activities of the Cato Manor police squad, exposed by this newspaper last December. Our motives and professionalism have also been questioned.'

In what the *Sunday Times* said was 'again' separating 'truth from fiction', Dlamini confirmed what the state had said in court: the investigation was complete. They had 'uncovered startling evidence' that people who weren't suspects had been killed by the Cato Manor Organised Crime Unit; scenes had been tampered with, witnesses threatened, weapons planted and cases opened after the deceased had been killed.

Dlamini expressed dismay at the public support for the policemen, asking if there were different standards for the 'heroes of Cato Manor'. They barged into suspects' homes, but complained in court and to the media about being arrested in front of their friends and families at home?

> What is not said is that the deceased's homes were raided in the middle of the night and they were never given the courtesy of being arrested. Instead they were allegedly killed after they had surrendered. What is ignored is that members of the Cato Manor Unit were not arrested for putting dangerous criminals behind bars. Instead these officers face 71 charges including murder.

Johan thought what was ignored was that Cato Manor hadn't been dealing with courteous people – they were murder and robbery suspects – and that they had arrested many suspects who had been prosecuted and were serving jail time. Moses Dlamini, he thought, had been caught up in the hype.

Why would IPID, an organisation tasked with ensuring the independent oversight of SAPS, write a one-sided commentary for the Sunday Times?

The 18 Cato Manor officers, facing multiple murder charges, were given bail and went back to work.

•

In mid-July 2012 Johan was having dinner at an Asian restaurant in Durban North. It was a regular haunt – the waiter, Shortie, always brought him 'Joe-han's salad – a salmon and avocado combo – without him having to ask. He was chatting to the owner, Liu, when in walked an advocate from the Durban branch of the Asset Forfeiture Unit (AFU). He called Johan over. He wanted to give him a heads up. Both SARS and the AFU had been told to investigate Johan's finances, to conduct a lifestyle audit and check what properties he owned. They were looking for evidence of irregular income. They hadn't been able to find anything so had checked his petrol claims at work. No irregularities there either.

Johan thought they sounded desperate.

They must have been, with Police Minister Nathi Mthethwa breathing down their necks. But I felt uneasy: I'd also been phoned by a journalist asking for comment on information she had received that I was to be charged with racketeering.

Johan had assured her she must've been misinformed.

Racketeering was serious stuff. I'd been on two training courses with US prosecutor Michael Johnson, who had helped draft South African racketeering legislation. It's designed to neutralise crime syndicates and carries a fine of a million rand or life imprisonment. I knew the exact requirements.

It involved proving the existence of a criminal enterprise either by having an insider from within the enterprise, legally intercepting communications between gang members or by having an agent planted within the enterprise to prove an ongoing pattern of criminality.

Proving a case of racketeering without this kind of evidence is very difficult. I had successfully managed two racketeering investigations – one involving human trafficking, the other narcotics. I couldn't see how they could pin racketeering charges on a general and an entire police unit, who could well have been performing their mandated function.

But clearly the acting national director of public prosecutions didn't see it the same way.

The authorisation request to prosecute for racketeering was signed by KZN prosecution head Moipone Noko on 16 August 2012 and must've landed on her boss Nomgcobo Jiba's desk in Pretoria shortly thereafter, because she signed it the following day. Booysen and Cato Manor were to be prosecuted for racketeering. Evidence that would take Johan and a team weeks to study, she dispensed with in a day.

The general procedure is for the local prosecutor, in this case Noko, as well as the investigating officer, to travel to Pretoria to do a detailed presentation. If details are missing they are sent back. Not in this case. Jiba could not have applied her mind. She just signed.

- 14 -
ARRESTED

On the morning of 22 August Johan was driving in Durban North on his way to meet his attorney, when he got a call from a Colonel Pharasa Ncube, who worked on Mabula's team.

'General, I need to see you.'

'What for?' he asked. Ncube was cagey, so Johan asked: 'Do you want to arrest me?'

'Yes,' came the answer.

'Where would you like to meet?'

'Where can we meet?'

'At my office.'

Once again, Johan thought, a colonel had been sent by a general to come and do his dirty work. He went back to his office and told his staff that he was about to be arrested. Two of them started crying. Deena Govender, who had brought Madhoe to the Elangeni Hotel for the meeting that caused all the trouble, was particularly agitated. Johan told them to calm down and went to sit in his boardroom. Alone.

Half an hour passed. No Colonel Ncube.

After a while someone from the Special Task Force contacted Johan to say the arrest was imminent. He sounded apologetic – the Task Force is an elite force, used for terrorist and hostage situations. Johan prepared himself for amateur dramatics.

Within the hour, they arrived, dressed in combat gear and armed with pistols. He almost laughed as Ncube handed him a warrant for his arrest.

Johan asked him for the founding affidavit. Ncube looked confused.

'What?'

The founding affidavit – there must be a written statement detailing the intended charges?

'Oh …'

Realising he wasn't going to get much information out of Ncube, Johan told him they should get to court as soon as possible, so he could apply for bail. The court closed at 4pm. Johan didn't want to spend the night in the cells.

To Johan's astonishment, Ncube called for cable ties to handcuff him.

Is this necessary? You have an armed Task Force with you.

'I must comply with regulations.'

What regulations?

'Just regulations.'

Johan thought it seemed as if the instruction from above was to make a meal of it. Johan climbed into the lift, handcuffed. A cleaner stared at him, surprised. Downstairs, Johan was escorted into a waiting car. The Task Force member who had phoned him sat next to him. Johan knew him – they had done operations together. Johan thought that he looked embarrassed.

As the car got on the South Coast highway to Amanzimtoti, Johan could see a convoy of cars behind them, including Deena Govender's. He insisted on accompanying Johan. 'Anything could happen,' Govender said.

At home Johan's domestic worker looked perplexed. She had just chased away some journalists. Now her employer walked in with his hands bound. Govender kept the journalists at bay outside.

They searched his house, for what Johan wasn't sure. When they took him into his bedroom, Colonel Ncube asked for his firearm. His handcuffs were removed.

My firearm is on my ankle – it's always on my ankle.

Ncube said: 'Ooh – you could've shot us!'

Yes – you should've searched me for my firearm. That was the regulation you should've been concerned with.

They put his firearm in a clear plastic bag. Just before they stepped outside, the handcuffs were put on again. Johan wondered what regulation that was.

Next stop was the Air Wing at the old Durban airport. Mabula and representatives from IPID would be there along with eight other Organised Crime members – six from Cato Manor and two from Port Shepstone. The 18 who had been given bail in June were due back in court the next day – so all 30 accused would appear together for the first time.

The Air Wing is a protected area with high security; Johan had never seen the huge steel gates open before. But today they were wide open for dozens of journalists and cameras.

He was relieved they took him through the back entrance. Once inside, a special task force member told him that General Mabula had just arrived and was annoyed that they hadn't brought Johan through the front gates where the media had gathered.

Johan went to speak to Mabula and asked him the reason for the show.

'It's not me,' Mabula said, 'it's IPID,' implying that they were in charge of the operation. Johan, handcuffs removed, went to talk to Glen Angus from IPID. He agreed it wasn't necessary at all; Mabula had insisted.

Johan sat in an office while they completed the paperwork: statements, fingerprints, mug shots and constitutional rights forms. Colonel Ncube seemed to be taking forever, redoing forms, starting again. Johan was sure he was procrastinating so they wouldn't get to court in time to apply for bail.

Finally it was finished and time to leave for the cells. IPID's Angus told Johan he could hide his face before the barrage of press outside, offering to put Johan's jacket over his head. Johan gave him a withering look.

Angus was meant to be a neutral investigator – but it seemed to me that he was reveling in the theatrics. IPID was the police watchdog – but Angus was allowing a circus. I told him I had never hidden my face in my life and was definitely not going to do it now.

He turned to his eight co-accused and said: *Do you want to hide your faces?*

'No, sir,' came the reply.

Johan walked out first, handcuffed again, to a waiting car. It was getting dark, making the camera flashes and lights even brighter. As they pulled off, there was a tap on the car window. It was an SABC journalist.

'*Hamba kahle*, Booysen,' she shouted. 'Go well!'

On their arrival at the Durban North Police Station, Johan was surprised to see crowds of support. Among them was Hillcrest resident Penny Katz who had started a Facebook page to support the unit. She had even had T-shirts printed. On the back were the words: I SUPPORT THE DURBAN SERIOUS VIOLENT CRIMES UNIT; on the front was the picture that the *Sunday Times* had described as a 'post-kill party'.

Penny is a fiery, outspoken redhead.

'Why shouldn't they have a drink?' she'd said after seeing the picture. 'If I had to do the job they did, I would too, just to celebrate being alive. These guys helped so many people – now we want to help them, pay it forward. We will be in court every time they appear. Unit means unity – and we're with them.'

By the looks of it, the unit wouldn't be eating prison fare that night; apart from posters and messages of support, there were takeaways of every description, flasks of coffee and blankets.

They walked in, down to the cells. Their shoelaces and ties were removed.

Johan had slipped his phone in his shoe. He didn't want to lose contact. Earlier he'd got hold of his family to tell them he'd been arrested. His daughter, Natalie, had been in tears. For the first time since the whole fiasco began, he felt emotional.

He found a newspaper and laid it out on the grubby mattress in his cell. He was still in his suit. From next door someone chirped: 'You're going to be all over the papers!'

There was an interleading door where the other accused were eating the takeaways. Mukesh Panday, Eugene van Tonder, Vincent Auerbach, Asogram Pillay, Bongani Zondi, Charles Smith, Musa Nkabane and Nico Crouse – men he usually saw at crime scenes – were now sharing a cell, along with a bottle of whisky, which they were trying to hide from him. He was still the general, captive or not.

I'll have some too, he said, and took a swig. It was going to be long night.

Early the next morning, Johan's brother Marius brought him some clean clothes and he went to the police barracks to have a shower. Willie Olivier, who had appeared a month earlier and was out on bail, arrived and told Johan he had arranged for them to use a tunnel between the courtroom and the holding cells so they didn't have to face the media.

No, said Johan. *Let's go out and face them. I'm here because I'm fighting crime, not doing crime.*

He was glad they did. The support was comforting.

A tow-truck company had parked its entire fleet outside the magistrate's court. People wearing Penny's T-shirts were carrying homemade posters, one reading: 'Never give up, never give in, fight for what's right, fight till you win.'

Inside, magistrates and prosecutors came to wish them well. There were people in every corner of the court – on laps, on the floor, standing shoulder to shoulder. Some had brought fistfuls of cash to help with bail. Johan had never seen anything like it before.

In a way the show the investigators had made of our arrests had backfired. Now we had support from all quarters. Money was pouring in for our defence.

Carl van der Merwe was administering a trust fund to pay bail and future legal fees; the daily rate of advocates is more than most people earn in a month.

In later months, at a fundraiser auction, Springbok fullback André Joubert's 1995 winning World Cup blazer would add R50 000 to the kitty. The businessman who bought it presented it to Johan. André Joubert did the handover and put it over his shoulders. Johan was moved.

For once I was lost for words.

In court, the 30 officers filed in: 28 from Organised Crime and two from the National Intervention Unit, who'd been involved in the Bongani Mkhize shooting.

There were 116 charges by then. Counts 1 and 2 were contraventions of the Organised Crime Act: managing an enterprise through a pattern of racketeering activity and participating in the conduct of an enterprise through a pattern of racketeering. The rest of the charges ranged from murder, housebreaking, theft and intent to do grievous bodily harm to contravening the Firearms Control Act and obstructing and defeating the course of justice.

Accused number 1 was Johan Wessel Booysen, the manager of the enterprise. According to IPID's Dlamini, even though he hadn't been physically present, he had aided and abetted Cato Manor: 'As leader of the unit at provincial level, he ought to have known that what the unit members were doing was wrong and taken steps thereof.'

Nonsense, Johan thought.

I had last been a unit commander in 1995 and had since been stationed at HQ. In March 2010 I had been appointed head of the Hawks. Yet I was being charged for shootings that happened at Organised Crime in 2011. I was never in direct command of any Organised Crime unit during the period covered by the indictment.

Even though Colonel Rajen Aiyer had been in direct commander of Cato Manor, Dlamini said there was no evidence linking him to the case: 'We will not be using him as a witness.'

But in defending the authorisation to prosecute Booysen, Advocate Jiba said she had relied on the statements of Aiyer and two other witnesses. Witnesses who, Johan thought, would come to be used by the state.

They were a police informer called Ndlondlo; and a police reservist, Aris Danikas. I call them the state's useful idiots.

- 15 -

THE WITNESSES WHO WEREN'T

DANIKAS

In 1998, when Johan needed to buy a new computer, his friend Willie Olivier told him to try an electronics shop in downtown Durban, run by Aris Danikas, a Greek national. His prices were good and he had plenty of patience with the techno illiterate.

Johan and Danikas became friends over the years.

He was an amusing guy – hyperactive and enthusiastic. We developed a relationship – he was interested in policing. He'd phone me if a computer was brought into his shop that he thought had been stolen and he later signed up to become a police reservist. He had a brother in Athens who was a cop.

A few years later Johan and his then teenage daughter Natalie popped in to see Danikas at his shop – and it was in the throes of being robbed. Unbeknownst to them as they walked into the front of the shop, four armed men were in the process of stealing laptops and had taken Danikas' gun. As Johan and his daughter entered, they were forced into a backroom where Danikas and Zonke, his business partner, were being held. Johan didn't want to try any heroics with Natalie there so he passed his gun to Danikas as the robbers fled. Danikas chased after them and fired a shot, wounding one of the men.

In the weeks ahead, I took flak for having handed over my firearm to a civilian, but I was cleared by a departmental inquiry.

There were a few reservists attached to specialised units. Danikas wanted to be one of these, so Johan pulled some strings and got him seconded to Organised Crime. The Cato Manor guys found him a bit irritating, but occasionally took him out with them on an investigation.

One night in April 2007 Danikas and Johan were having dinner when a call came in from radio control. Cato Manor's Mossie Mostert and Eugene van Tonder had been involved in a shoot-out. They had been tipped off about a robbery in Malvern in Queensburgh. The robbers were going to pounce on the owner of the local Nando's as he got home with the takings. Instead, the two Cato Manor detectives arrived before the robbers, who drove straight into the garage where Mostert and Van Tonder were waiting. One robber was shot dead; another was wounded. A third fled.

By the time Johan got there, Mostert and Van Tonder had called an ambulance for the critically wounded robber. Danikas, said Johan, began behaving like a drama queen and began filming on his cellphone.

He kept shouting: 'Director, director, we must call an ambulance!'

Danikas thought they should resuscitate the bleeding robber. Johan was annoyed.

I wasn't going to do that and risk contracting HIV or hepatitis. Nor was he. The ambulance took 38 minutes to get there. This was a situation the rest of us had been in many times. And many times the tables would have been turned – with an officer lying dead or dying.

After that Johan was less inclined to take Danikas along with him.

He behaved like he was directing an action movie, instead of shutting up and keeping out of the way.

Danikas must have sensed that he was being excluded. The following year, when a fellow reservist told him he was to be promoted to a captain, he reacted badly. What about him? He phoned Johan, who told him it could have been an affirmative action appointment. Next thing Johan knew, it was in the newspaper.

DAILY NEWS
29 AUGUST 2008
RESERVIST MAY RESIGN OVER PROMOTION ROW
Police reservist Aris Danikas, who claims to have recovered stolen property worth R1.5 million, personally arrested 139 suspects, as well as recovered stolen cars and firearms, has had enough. As a reservist, he has the right to be paid for his efforts, but has never taken a cent, doing what he does for the love of his adopted country.

Danikas, who hails from Greece, is a qualified electronic engineer specialising in computers, and has a shop in Durban.

Danikas was quoted in the newspaper report as saying that he had recently recovered a laptop belonging to Malusi Gigaba, then deputy minister of home affairs, and that he often gave presentations to the police on how to detect stolen computer hardware. He believed he was an asset to the force.

The newspaper was sympathetic. 'Yet he has remained at the rank of sergeant,' the journalist wrote. 'He believes that by now, in view of his contribution to crime fighting, he should be a captain. But he has been told by senior officers that he will never be promoted because he is white.'

Johan was annoyed when he read the article.

Apart from the fact that it brought the SAPS into disrepute, Danikas had lied. He wasn't a qualified engineer – he had done an elementary course at Natal Tech. Nor were reservists ever paid – they were community volunteers. And he was hardly an asset to the force – only one person he'd arrested had ever been convicted in court – and he'd given a single lecture to police on how to find owner particulars on stolen computers.

Johan suspended Danikas. He sent someone round to his house to retrieve his state-issued firearm. Danikas resigned. He remonstrated with Johan, telling him he felt degraded and humiliated, particularly as he'd had to give up his gun in front of his fiancée.

A few months later, in November 2008, Johan had a call from Danikas' business partner, Zonke. Something was amiss. Had he seen Danikas?

Johan went round and found a worried Zonke. She said Danikas had told her he was going to refurbish the shop and she should take a week off. On her return she'd found the shop empty but for empty computer boxes and Danikas' car keys on the counter. His phone was switched off.

Zonke assumed the worst: the stock had been stolen, Aris had been killed and his body was in the boot of his car, dumped somewhere.

Hardly, with the keys on the counter, thought Johan. He found the car in the parking garage. But no sign of Danikas, until a text message a day later: 'Mitso – Had to run like a goat. My father is sick and the situation in the country had become too difficult. You and Commissioner Brown are welcome to visit me in Greece.'

Danikas had gapped it, leaving behind a mountain of debt and a devastated Zonke. She had invested R300 000 in the business and feared she'd never see it again.

In early 2009 Johan had an email from Danikas. Johan reckoned his fiancée Shelley must have written it because the English was more understandable than Danikas'.

In it, he said he was disappointed in me. I had let him down. He had wined and dined me and helped me make important arrests, without which I would never have got to where I was in the police.

Johan thought Danikas had lost it.

This was confirmed when I heard from a mutual friend, an orthopod, who was also Greek, that Aris had wanted him to sign insurance papers, stating that he had health problems and could no longer work and should get a payout. The health problem was 'floaters' in his eyes, which supposedly affected computer work. The orthopod had refused to sign. Other Greek ex-pats told me they called Aris 'anypotaktos' – a draft dodger. He'd come to South Africa to avoid military service in Greece, they said, then tried to compensate by becoming a police reservist.

When creditors began circling, Danikas had hastily married Shelley, a South African, so she could get a Greek passport. It had puzzled Johan when Danikas had told him.

He said that one of his workers, who was a lay preacher and marriage officer, had married them in his flat. It was all very hush-hush. I couldn't understand it because it wasn't like him. A low-key wedding didn't fit the image he portrayed. Once they'd fled the country, it made sense.

A few months later, Danikas sent Johan pictures of his grand Greek wedding to Shelley – bride and groom strolling on the beach – and, in September 2011, pictures of their baby boy. He also wrote to the orthopod, telling him to leave South Africa before it went down the tubes.

Then, out of the blue in 2012, Danikas posted on YouTube a video with the caption: 'police torture of a suspect in durban s.africa'.

In it, several unidentified people stand around a bound and naked man, his head covered. According to Danikas, the man had tried to sell him a laptop, stolen in a car hijacking, so he had phoned Cato Manor, who took the suspect in for questioning. Danikas went along. He said officers had tortured the suspect until he led them to his accomplice – and to the stolen car.

In November 2015 Danikas would tell the *Sunday Times*, in an article promoting an Al Jazeera documentary called 'Echoes of Apartheid' – on extrajudicial killings in post-Apartheid South Africa – that he had shown Johan the video and that he had said: '... that's how we get confessions. We get the job done.'

In an earlier article, which was published on 24 February 2013, Danikas had told the *Sunday Times* he had decided to spill the beans after several attempts to contact him in Europe by 'suspicious people directly or indirectly involved with the Cato Manor case ... in order to protect myself, I have decided to go public as well as approach the local authorities for help'.

The article detailed Danikas' claims about the unit: 'A police reservist formerly embedded in the notorious Cato Manor Organised Crime Unit has become the first insider to publicly break ranks on the alleged "hit squad", spilling the beans – in a series of exclusive interviews with the *Sunday Times* – on the trail of torture and murder he says he witnessed.'

After that article, Danikas told the *Sunday Times* in April 2013 about an incident in 'a Durban township' in 2001. He said he was with more than a dozen policemen who had kicked down the door of a home, dragged a man out of a house and shot him, claiming he had lunged for a gun. But there had been no gun, said Danikas.

'I saw the guy being dragged out in his underwear,' he told the paper. 'Where could you put the gun? Up his arse? And with 12 armed police officers standing around him? There's no way there was a gun there.'

Soon afterwards, Danikas said, Johan had strolled over to congratulate his men on a job well done, 'as he always did after they shot someone'.

But Johan says he wasn't even there.

Surely the members of the Independent Complaints Directorate who attended would've reported seeing me if I was? Furthermore, Aris never even mentioned this incident in his statement to the NPA – why would he not have included this? I assumed he was mixing up incidents, adding his own version and feeding them to the Sunday Times.

According to Danikas, Cato Manor's 'standard policy' was to wait for a suspect to arrive at a scene then shoot to kill.

'They did not want any prisoners, because the system was corrupted and they would be out on bail,' he explained. He described the unit as 'trigger-happy people that have no respect for human life. They torture, use excessive, brutal force and alter evidence on a crime scene. This I witnessed myself first-hand.'

He told the newspaper that the Cato Manor 'death squad' and its nonchalant commander 'chilled him to the bone'. After the shoot-out in the garage in Malvern, he said, Johan had waited for the wounded robber to 'die like a dog'.

Yet, says Johan again, none of this was in Danikas' statement that the NPA was relying on.

What also puzzled me is that despite saying I chilled him to the bone he kept up regular correspondence with me – and my family. We received holiday photos from Paris and Christmas greetings from Athens.

Danikas was, Johan decided, a melodramatic fantasist.

And too much of a narcissist to come back to South Africa to be humiliated in the witness box and he would have been, because his statement in no way advanced the state's case. It contradicted what he had told the Sunday Times. *I later found out that he had dictated it to a South African lawyer over the phone. It wasn't even signed or dated.*

Danikas had left South Africa in 2008 – yet the indictment against Cato Manor stemmed from shootings that he hadn't attended, or when he had already left the country.

State advocate and lead prosecutor Sello Maema said as much in a letter to Danikas' lawyer, Julian Knight: 'The incidents that Danikas refers to in his draft statement started in 2001 to 2007, a period not covered in the indictment [which begins covering the period of 2008 onwards]. Most of those incidents are not referred to in the indictment and do not have dockets which relate to them.'

At best Danikas would be able to corroborate a pattern of behaviour by Cato Manor, but there was no evidence of racketeering. He was, said Maema, a risky witness: 'We are not sure that the witness is telling us everything, the chances of surprises in court are very real ... a very risky consideration to expect him to come to South Africa for the purposes of testifying.'

Yet the NPA's Nomgcobo Jiba seemed to regard him as a trump card, says Johan.

Such was the paucity of witnesses, it seemed, that she even took seriously Colonel Rajen Aiyer.

AIYER

'I found Colonel Aiyer to be a dismal witness ...'

So said Advocate Nazeer Cassim in 2014 after he had conducted Johan's disciplinary hearing. SAPS had charged Johan with misconduct for failing to act against a unit under his direct command.

At the hearing, held in a boardroom in Sandton, Johan was at pains to point out that the unit wasn't under his direct command. It was under the command of Colonel Rajen Aiyer and according to SAPS regulations 'it is the responsibility of the Unit Commander and not the Provincial Commander to institute appropriate disciplinary steps ...'

But Aiyer, an SAPS witness, told Chairman Cassim that Johan controlled and undermined him, rendering him ineffective.

Johan and his lawyer, Van der Merwe, drew the chairman's attention to a newspaper report after a Cato Manor drugs raid in Chatsworth in which Aiyer had taken ownership of the unit. He had been quoted in the *Daily News* on the 10 October 2008 as saying 'We want the public to know that Provincial Commissioner Hamilton Ngidi is determined to rid society of its rotten elements and will not back down. I am very proud of the work my members have been doing.'

And they supplied to the hearing the minutes of an Organised Crime Unit meeting Aiyer had chaired in December 2008, outlining his 'expectations' for 2009: 'I am the Unit Commander here and what I say goes. No one can challenge me, those who have tried and went that route, I have forgiven them. In 2009 those who don't follow protocol can jump in the lake.'

Aiyer told Advocate Cassim that he'd tried time and time again to take control, but Johan victimised him, bugged his phone conversations, visited Cato Manor without his knowledge and went to crime scenes without his permission.

Johan and Aiyer had had countless run-ins over the years.

They were mainly because he kept saying defamatory things about me. I once heard from a source that he accused me of being part of a 'Big Five assassination squad' and of plotting to kill Schabir Shaik.

Shaik was then doing prison time for having a corrupt relationship with President Zuma. Just why Johan would want to kill Shaik wasn't clear, so he asked his source to find out. In a recorded phone conversation in which the source pretended to be one of Shaik's brothers, Aiyer mouthed off:

The head of the detective services is Brown. Below him is Booysen. Now these two 'wit ous' [white guys] are running the show. They've been running it since '99. All these are right-wingers, ex-Rhodesians. They've been working at Murder and Robbery – they've been killing our people. Let me tell you, all these deaths that are taking place, all these armed robberies, I don't want to go into that, because that's another chapter. And Bheki Cele is also in with it now.

The person pretending to be Yunis Shaik asks: 'Who? Who's these guys?'

To which Aiyer replies: 'The Cato Manor office. The Serious and Violent Crime at Cato Manor. It's falling under me, but can you imagine, I am the unit commander and I have no control over these fuckers ... Boss, let me tell you, the Cato Manor office, the Serious and Violent Crime office must be shut down.'

The person pretending to be Yunis Shaik follows with: 'No, we will put you in control. I've heard about these guys calling themselves the Big Five.'

Johan had never heard of the Big Five, but according to Aiyer, he was the leader of this rogue gang. Pat Brown and Willie Olivier were also members.

And Aiyer elaborates: 'The head of the Big Five is Booysen, Johan Booysen ... The Big Five here ... big money! They've got billions of it. You know all these armed robberies that are happening here? Where's the money going? Booysen is stealing it and a security company run by Booysen's brother ... Boss, you know what ... I'm next in line to head the Scorpions, the new DPCI in KZN.'

Why the state would consider Aiyer a credible witness was considered a mystery to many who knew him.

He'd been called the exact opposite in a magistrate's court, when standing as a witness against a gang of robbers. Aiyer had fallen victim to the gang while off-duty and sitting in his car with a girlfriend. Both had reported the incident, but Aiyer had drafted her statement for her. Neither gave defining features of the suspects, other than that one of them was barefoot.

A few weeks later, there was a shooting involving a gang in the same area that Aiyer had been robbed. He rushed to the scene and started taking videos and photographs, before being chased away by detectives who said he was interfering.

Back at the office, Aiyer changed his original statement to fit the description of the suspects. No longer was the robber barefoot, he was wearing trainers, just like a suspect he'd seen in the latest robbery. But he'd left his girlfriend's statement as it was.

In court he was accused of '... defeating justice by having a statement typed for his girlfriend ... who had no knowledge of the contents ...'

The magistrate said: 'As a judicial officer, it is my preference that should Colonel Aiyer have any matters in this court, that matters ought not to proceed where he is a witness ... in short the credibility and reliability of Colonel Aiyer leaves much to be desired.'

Advocate Nazeer Cassim didn't think he had credibility either, saying his evidence was 'unpersuasive':

> He is obsessed by the notion of his own importance and his entire testimony was permeated by his political acceptability and self-importance ... I think those in charge of the SAPS ought to carefully consider Colonel Aiyer's continued role in the police force ... His affidavit ... is punctuated by invective and pure hatred for Booysen. He is obsessed by the notion that there is a vendetta to have him killed – to the extent that he is paranoid. I can find no substance in this speculative realm of make believe.

Cassim questioned the SAPS' motive in calling Aiyer as a witness against Johan:

> If in fact the employer actually believed it could establish a case against the employee based on the evidence of Colonel Aiyer, this was a serious error of judgement and, worse still, a strong indication that the employer sought to create a case where one did not exist.

It seemed that was precisely what the state was doing too.

NDLONDLO

Cato Manor detective Mossie Mostert had an informer called Bheki Mthiyane, who owned taxis. He'd met him in Stanger in 2009. His informer name was Ndlondlo. He was a slippery character, but gave Mostert useful information about criminal elements that often led to arrests:

> He had a criminal record for stealing a car, but in my dealings with him he was reliable. Informers are a necessary part of policing, but don't always give you results. Ndlondlo did. He helped us solve a massacre at Ntuzuma, when six people, one of them a radio presenter, were shot dead at a party on Christmas Day 2009. For that information he got R50 000. There were risks, but it was worth his while.

One day in March 2012, after Mabula and his team had begun the investigation into Cato Manor, Ndlondlo had phoned Mostert in a state. He said he'd been receiving anonymous phone calls, saying that they knew he was an informer for Cato Manor. He was worried that if his cover was blown, he'd be expelled from his taxi association and everyone would know that he was an *impimpi* (spy). His life would be in danger – the *izinkabi* would be after him. Mostert, a bear of a man, told him bluntly to ignore them:

> I told him to tell them to fuck off, but he was rattled. So I got my wife, who worked at Telkom, to trace the number and found that it came from the ICD office in Durban. Then we recorded the next conversation. It was clear from the recordings they were trying to get him to implicate Cato Manor, putting words in his mouth.

Mostert got Ndlondlo to write a statement:

> Unknown people are phoning me ... they said Mossie and Cato Manor 'are fuck all and I must not worry about them anymore'. This shows that they know I was an informant for Mossie and Cato Manor who the criminals fear. Criminals and gangsters from Joeberg [*sic*] are scared to come to KZN because of Cato Manor.
>
> The phone caller said that he knows that I was the informant for Mossie and that whenever Mossie killed someone I used to throw the firearm at the dead person. The calls were already made three times to me.
>
> I desperately need help to get out of this situation.

Colonel Hoosen from Organised Crime forwarded the statement and a covering letter to the ICD:

> COMPLAINT OF UNETHICAL CONDUCT re REPORT FROM INFORMANT
>
> This office received a report from a registered informant who raised concerns about certain phone calls he received, which he

believes may have possibly compromised him as an informant for the Police.

The ... informant ... reported that an unknown person called on three different occasions from a number 031310300 which appeared on his screen.

The caller ... told him that he knew he had planted guns on deceased victims on behalf of his handler.

The informant sought assistance from this office because he believes that his life and that of his family may be in danger.

The methods that the caller used are unethical and unbecoming of any investigating officer and not in the interests of justice.

Two other of Mostert's informers had also been contacted and asked to turn against Cato Manor. They had told the caller where to get off. But Ndlondlo was vulnerable. His taxis had been impounded and he was desperate.

The investigators apparently used this to win Ndlondlo over. According to Ndlondlo's wife, Brigadier Mokoena had told him she would get his taxis back for him if he made a statement against Cato Manor. She also said they had promised him medical treatment – he'd suffered a stroke and had AIDS.

In a garbled second statement, Ndlondlo named taxi association members he said he'd heard had paid Cato Manor members and 'Big Boss Booysen' for killing industry rivals.

It was, thought Johan, a desperate attempt to invent evidence.

Ndlondlo had only become Mossie's informer in 2009 – after Chonco's death. He was never an informer in the Chonco case. So he provided hearsay evidence, which is admissible in racketeering cases if there's good reason why the source cannot give evidence. But the investigators never bothered to get in touch with Ndlondlo's source, who would have been the actual witness. They coerced Ndlondlo into making wild allegations.

Ndlondlo stated that Magojela Ndimande's death on the N3 had netted Cato Manor R750 000. Two taxi members – Bongizwe Mhlongo and Zanele Zondi – had delivered the cash to 'Boss Booysen'. Zanele, the statement read, was one of Booysen's registered informers: 'Always when

Zanele and Bongizwe left with money they would tell us that the money was going to be given to the boss, referring to Mr Booysen and they would say "we have connection" and they would pay Mr Booysen as head.'

The killing of Bongani Mkhize on Umgeni Road had earned Cato Manor a million, he said. Just to confuse matters further, Ndlondlo said that he'd been told that Inkosi Zondi, the former policeman and relative of President Jacob Zuma, and for whose death Bongani Mkhize had been sought, had been in on the racket, as he worked at Cato Manor.

'Nkosi [sic] Zondi arranged with his unit Cato Manor and also Booysen his commander,' Ndlondlo claimed. 'I was there when the money was arranged to pay Cato Manor for well job done ... [sic]. We were told feedback that Nkosi [sic] Zondi was paid the money.'

Zondi had worked at Cato Manor long before the killings for which the unit was being indicted. Whoever had taken Ndlondlo's statement hadn't even done the basics, Johan thought.

At the time of Colonel Chonco's death in 2008, Inkosi Zondi had been gone from Cato Manor for seven years. So whoever took Ndlondlo's statement had taken some real facts and threaded them with lies in order to try to prove a nonexistent case.

Richard Ramukosi, the investigator who'd taken the statement, had once been a *'kitskonstabel'*, a breed of policeman in the apartheid era known more for their zeal than skill, in Johan's opinion.

If Ndlondlo had told him that Zanele Zondi had paid me, why didn't he go and get a statement from him? And if Zanele Zondi was my informer, why didn't he check the SAPS database to see if he really was? The truth is he was never an informer. Ramukosi didn't even try to trace him or Bongizwe Mhlongo to find out about paying me these so-called millions over the years to kill taxi owners. Why? I think because he was acting under instruction from Mabula and Mokoena and they knew it wouldn't support their narrative.

Zanele Zondi and Bongizwe, via their lawyer, complained to the national head of the Hawks and to Cato Manor lead prosecutor Sello Maema that Ndlondlo's statement was fictitious: 'The allegations contained therein could be objectively proved by any serious investigator of crime to be nothing but patent falsehoods. All the allegations made in this statement can never stand the scrutiny of a court of law. Ndlondlo is now deceased and can never take the stand and be discredited.'

Ndlondlo had been put into witness custody in Mpumalanga, where he died in November 2012.

He never got the medical treatment promised to him. His wife said his impounded taxis were never returned. In an affidavit, she said she didn't believe her husband had either written or dictated his second statement. Johan didn't believe it either.

It was a ridiculous attempt by Mabula and company to find a witness against us. To make it worse, Cato Manor prosecutor Sello Maema falsely claimed in an affidavit that Ndlondlo had been killed. He had actually died of natural causes while in protective custody. I later laid perjury charges against Advocate Maema for persisting with that lie. And what did it matter that Ndlondlo was dead? If Maema believed his story, why didn't he ask the investigators to go and corroborate it with Zanele Zondi? Instead they went with a statement from a dead man. They could find no one to prove that Cato Manor had been hired guns – or that I had pulled the strings from behind my desk at HQ.

I began wondering on what exactly the state was basing its case against us. There certainly didn't seem to be any evidence.

- 16 -

THE EVIDENCE THAT WASN'T

Two weeks after appearing in court, the Cato Manor members were suspended. Deputy National Police Commissioner Magda Stander recommended their suspensions the day before she retired from 41 years of service with SAPS. She had also over the years, as head of Human Resources, approved awards for them.

Now these awards were listed in the murder charges against them: Cato Manor officers had killed for money, read the charge sheet: 'In some of their killings, the unlawful activities were motivated by the desire to enrich themselves through state monetary awards and/or certificates for excellent performance and financial benefits from associations and/or business and/or individuals in conflict with the deceased.'

The gist of the state's case was that Johan had managed a team of police officers who had, over a three-year period, murdered 28 people; broken into their homes to kill them; planted unlicensed firearms to create the impression that they'd been armed and stolen items of value and cash from the deceased and their families. Then they'd either claimed for SAPS awards or been paid by rival taxi groups. Johan noted that there was no additional detail about these alleged payments.

They had chosen 28 cases of the myriad that Cato Manor had been involved in and decided that these constituted racketeering. And decided that I had been in on the deal, but there was no clarity on exactly how. During the same period, 2008 to 2011, the Cato Manor Unit had arrested more than 400 serious and violent offenders. There was no clarity in the dockets on why, if they had acted as assassins, they'd killed certain individuals and not others. If it was for money, what payment had they received apart from the police awards, which had been approved by their superiors?

Six of the murder charges were directly related to the killing of Lieutenant Colonel Chonco and three to the murder of Inkosi Zondi. One of these was Sifiso Ndimande, nephew of Magojela Ndimande. It was alleged that Cato Manor detectives Mossie Mostert, Neville Eva and Paddy Padayachee had travelled to Rustenburg, killed Ndimande and placed a firearm next to his body to create the impression he was armed.

Five charges were for the deaths of suspects in ATM bombings and a further 14, said the state, had been killed by Cato Manor without warrants of arrest, or tangible evidence. Count 94 was the 4 September 2011 death of former ANC branch chairman Qinisani Gwala, which had elicited high-profile inquiries at the time.

Gwala was allegedly wanted for questioning in connection with the 2010 murder of Eshowe policeman Kevin Marralich, who had been killed while out fishing with his girlfriend, who was raped and left for dead. Gwala lived at Esikhawini, 150 kilometres north of Durban, and was out on bail for an attempted hijacking. He had been attending tribal court at the Esikhawini community hall in September 2011 when the Cato Manor officers, including Mossie Mostert, arrived to question him. He told the officers they had the wrong person and took them to his home to get his ID. There, they said, he had fired at them through a window.

The state alleged he was handcuffed at the time Cato Manor police shot him and that they had planted a revolver next to his body. The state said Gwala's brother had been home but had been 'shoved into another house' and his head covered 'with a washing basin'. They didn't mention that, apart from the loaded .38 special found next to his body, in a later search of the premises the first responder, a constable, had found a pump-action shotgun under a mattress.

Then there was Kwazi Ndlovu. Count 66: 'During the early hours of 01 April 2010, the accused proceeded to the deceased's house. On arrival they broke open and entered the house of the complainants, fired shots and fatally wounded the deceased ... Kwazi Wiseboy Ndlovu, a 16-year-old male person.'

Ndlovu had, according to the state, been unarmed. Searching for escaped prisoners, Cato Manor officers claimed that the boy, lying on a couch, had pointed a weapon at them. This was disputed by a pathology report that indicated that the position of his body was 'not reconcilable with the usual position adopted in firing a weapon'. There was no evidence, said the state, that the teenager had posed a threat to the police. And the officer who'd fired the fatal shots, Paddy Padayachee, had mysteriously disappeared, supposedly 'to hospital'.

The scene was also contaminated and fingerprints on the firearm allegedly held by Ndlovu were fudged.

Johan had heard about the shooting on the news and phoned the commander at Organised Crime in Richards Bay, asking him to send someone to the scene. He'd reported back to Johan that IPID was there and that all was under control. Clearly it wasn't, as Johan later found out.

The standard procedure is for IPID to secure the shooting scene and to get fingerprints taken. Yet the deceased's alleged firearm was never fingerprinted. And they allowed people to run all over the show and contaminate the scene.

Now Johan was facing charges for not taking disciplinary measures against the officers involved in the shooting.

I was handling a multitude of other investigations at the time. Yet the state said that I should have acted against Cato Manor – not Colonel Aiyer, the Organised Crime unit commander, not the provincial commissioner. It was as if I had been present at the shooting scene. I hadn't.

Johan knew that they had to carefully scrutinise the dockets after the discovery process, the period during which the accused can evaluate the state's evidence against them.

He got a team of former Cato Manor detectives together to begin working through the 116 counts. Although he'd been charged, he wasn't familiar with any of the cases, apart from knowing who had been sought for Chonco's murder and why.

For six weeks they sat outside on his veranda in Toti from midday until 8 or 9pm, trawling through reports, postmortems and witness statements. Johan would read the statements aloud and they'd go through them, sentence by sentence: Shane Naidoo – who had dates at his fingertips; Mostert – able to remember names, faces and places; Raymond Lee, Jeremy Martins and Johnny Smith and Anton Lockem – were regulars. Lockem preferred plumbing to working on dockets so would find odd jobs around Johan's house. Other members of Cato Manor, like Willie Olivier, popped in when they were needed, or were phoned for details of cases they'd been involved in.

Johan thought they were a dream team.

I'd been managing cases for 30 years – the others had put away hundreds of criminals and been praised by High Court judges for the quality of their evidence and preparation.

But it all depended on the quality of the evidence against them.

After a few days it became clear that it was weak: the chain of evidence wasn't intact – statements from witnesses were missing or incomplete; some Cato Manor officers had been indicted even though there was no evidence they'd been at the scene; there were statements commissioned in conflicting locations, without the deponent present.

Whoever it was – one of the investigators – would take a statement then commission it later, so the location didn't match where and when the statement was made.

There was a firearm recovered from a crime scene that had only been entered into a register seven years later. Yet, says Johan, it was still included as evidence.

Whoever had attended the shooting had neglected to hand in the firearm at the time. This renders an exhibit useless at a trial – who says the gun is the same one? How many people used it in between?

Some witnesses had been duplicated – there were 241 – not 309 as listed. In some instances statements hadn't even been commissioned. Sloppy, thought Johan.

In one case, two different statements were filed in the docket from the same witness – but signed a year apart. Both were from the girlfriend of suspected bank robber, Prince Thabede. Her first statement had some circumstantial evidence that suggested Cato Manor officers had forced their way into Thabede's KwaMashu home, shot him and planted an unlicensed .38 revolver next to his body. Then, says Johan, the investigators had screwed it up.

For some reason they had done a second statement and added stuff, so that it was different to the first. We couldn't understand why they had – it was fatal to their investigation. Her signature was different too.

Initials on more than a dozen pages were wrong – as if the witness had forgotten her own initials. Johan got an accredited handwriting expert to examine the documents. He made an affidavit, saying on one of the statements was a forgery.

Sometimes, even the laboratory numbers conflicted.

Exhibits that had been sent to the lab with an identifying number had come back with a different number, so we knew they wouldn't pass muster in court. The doctrine of continuity of possession, an essential element of a case, had been compromised. How were they going to prove in court that they were the same exhibits?

In one case, the wrong projectiles were handed in as evidence – whoever had signed them out from the mortuary after the autopsy must've lost them, so gave investigators projectiles from another crime scene. But they didn't match those in the autopsy report, says Johan.

It didn't seem to concern lead investigator Jan Mabula or the prosecutors – they'd included the mismatched projectiles as exhibits anyway.

Johan knew the evidence fell far short of requirements for a successful prosecution.

This was a high-level investigation done by generals, brigadiers and colonels, but they'd managed to bugger it up. Any branch commander worth his or her salt would not have dared refer incomplete dockets to prosecutors for a decision. It was incompetence combined with the desire to pursue a nefarious agenda.

There was little new in the Bongani Mkhize case.

Ballistics tests done at the scene at the time had found that none of the bullet casings matched the gun found in his car. However, primer residue was found on Mkhize's hands and the duty officer who came to attend the scene said the muzzle showed signs of recently burnt gunpowder. The state ignored this.

The charges stated that accused number 2, Paddy Padayachee, as well as Adrian Stoltz, Raymond Lee, Thomas Dlamuka, Stanley Mfene and Sibongile Sikhulume, had contravened a court interdict, chased and shot

Mkhize, then placed a firearm with 'serial number obliterated' on the floor of his front passenger seat. The charges stated: 'The accused tempered [sic] with the crime scene by placing a firearm next to the body of the deceased to create an impression that the deceased was armed ...'

The *Sunday Times* had claimed in a report on 26 August 2012 that explosive 'new information' had come to light in the Mkhize case. Included in this information, 'contained in police memos, sworn statements and ballistics and pathology reports seen by the *Sunday Times*' was that Mkhize had been speaking on the phone to an intelligence official at the time he was being shot at. This, the report said, would've made it 'near impossible' for him to have been firing at police. Johan doubted the story.

No such statement was filed. Anyway, why would Mkhize be talking on the phone if he were being chased and shot at? And if he wanted to report that he was being shot at, why didn't he phone 10111?

Although there wasn't a statement from this intelligence official in the docket, there was one from a pedestrian who said he'd been walking on the opposite side of the road at the time of the Mkhize shooting, heard a noise, saw people scrambling and then saw police surrounding a black car.

The witness said a 'tall Indian policeman' with a firearm had instructed the occupant to 'get out of the fucking car'. He'd repeated the instruction. When the driver, who had his window open, opened the car door, the Indian policeman had shot him.

But a ballistics expert said that glass shards in the car's door rubbers suggested that the windows had been closed during the shooting. He had also said that there were no indications of any shots fired from inside the vehicle.

There was no evidence other than old ballistic and postmortem reports, which international experts had found to be inconclusive. Our attorney Carl van der Merwe had travelled abroad to consult blood-spatter and ballistic experts in Holland, England and Ireland.

In February 2012 the Mkhize family had brought a civil case against the minister of police. In his response, Nathi Mthethwa filed an affidavit, stating that Cato Manor officers had acted 'lawfully and reasonably' when they shot Mkhize. In preparing for the civil case, lawyers for Mkhize's family had asked for a copy of the docket from NPA advocate Sello Maema, but for some reason he refused to give it to them. Only after contempt of court proceedings were instituted against the NPA did they release the docket.

With the family's legal team now ready, the minister's team applied for a remand. But the judge had had enough of delays and ordered the case to begin, only to have the minister's advocate inform the court that he had no witnesses to call, as the Cato Manor members weren't prepared to give evidence.

The Mkhize's family advocate disagreed. Cato Manor had already filed statements so there was no reason why they shouldn't testify. The judge thought so too and Mkhize's family won the civil case against the minister.

Johan says it was a tricky situation:

If Cato Manor members had been subpoenaed to testify in the civil matter, which they weren't, they would have had legal representation and could have refused to answer possible incriminating questions. It was a Catch-22. To me it's unfortunate that they weren't subpoenaed and didn't testify in the civil case. Things could've turned out very differently.

In a move seen as paradoxically cementing his support of the Cato Manor officers, the minister applied for leave to appeal the court's finding, which was refused.

It was bizarre. On the one hand, you had the police minister arguing that Cato Manor had acted lawfully; on the other, the NPA saying the opposite in the racketeering court papers. The state even planned to call as a witness a new ballistics expert to say that Cato Manor had acted unlawfully.

•

In 2014 the ballistics expert, Captain Christian Mangena, would get a taste of what he might face in the witness stand in the Cato Manor racketeering case when he was called to give evidence at Johan's disciplinary. He was, says Johan, at a distinct disadvantage. His investigation had been done post facto and was reliant on photographs and old reports. His report was written in 2012; Mkhize was killed in 2009.

At the disciplinary, Van der Merwe cross-examined Mangena. Had he examined all the crime scene photographs – or only some of them? Had he read all the reports, or only the ones the investigators had given him? What about the primer residue on Mkhize's hand?

At a loss, Mangena had developed a 'cramp' in his leg and had hopped out of the room. Van der Merwe had used the opportunity to go the bathroom. He saw Mangena having a conversation on the phone at the end of the passage, cramp forgotten.

When they resumed, Van der Merwe asked him whether, given that tests had shown primer residue on Bongani Mkhize's hands, he could state conclusively that Mkhize hadn't fired his gun.

He said he could not. To Johan this was hugely significant.

Mangena made this concession under oath. This was the man the state planned to use as a witness when we went to trial.

It also had on its witness list IPID investigator Sharmilla Williams, who'd attended the Mkhize shooting. She would also testify at Johan's disciplinary hearing, saying there had been no evidence that Mkhize had fired at police, even though when she managed the crime scene, she hadn't had the gun tested for fingerprints.

When Van der Merwe asked her to explain why there had been primer residue on Mkhize's hand, she abruptly said she no longer wished to testify and asked Advocate Cassim to have her evidence struck off. She left the room and resigned from IPID a few months later; Cassim's findings in September 2014 excluded her evidence.

Primer residue had also been found on the hands of nine of the other deceased. In six of the cases, there had been inquests. Magistrates had found no evidence of wrongdoing by Cato Manor and the Directorate of Public Prosecutions had declined to prosecute them.

The prosecutors were now, Johan thought, riding roughshod over the Inquest Act.

In terms of the Inquest Act – section 17(a) – if an inquest is finalised and is to be reopened, the minister must request the Judge President of the province to appoint a judge to reopen that inquest. The Cato Manor prosecutors didn't do this.

•

At the end of the six-week process, Johan and the Cato Manor team had 379 pages of mistakes and irregularities.

In the 23 dockets of 500 pages, including attachments, Johan featured twice and was mentioned by three of the 290 witnesses, who confirmed his presence at crime scenes – after the action.

Nor was there damning evidence against Cato Manor. There was no direct evidence that they had planted firearms, there was only supposition. I'm not saying they were angels, but we live in a constitutional democracy and you need to prove your case. You can't build a case on supposition or manufactured evidence.

Yet Nomgcobo Jiba had authorised murder and racketeering charges. Even against accused number 28, Johnny Smith, who hadn't been a part of Cato Manor at the time of the alleged crimes. Johan wasn't sure why she'd given the go-ahead.

Either Jiba had been duped by the prosecutors and the investigators, or she had failed to apply her mind. Or she had authorised a prosecution because she'd been told to and wanted to protect certain people.

He suspected the latter.

The only explanation that I can conceive of is that the investigation into Thoshan Panday was sufficiently sensitive to cause me to tread on 'connected' toes. Hence the conflicting orders to cease/continue with the investigation. I believe that the earlier attempts to suspend me were part of attempts to get me out of the way.

Johan decided to take Jiba on. But not only her – the whole cabal within the criminal justice system that seemed so desperate to be rid of him.

- 17 -

BOOYSEN VS JIBA

DAILY NEWS
26 FEBRUARY 2014
CASE AGAINST BOOYSEN DROPPED
Durban – None of the information that the acting prosecutions boss, Nomgcobo Jiba, said she used in her decision to criminally charge Major General Johan Booysen has linked the suspended KwaZulu-Natal Hawks boss to the alleged offences.

This was one of the findings on Wednesday in the Durban High Court by Judge Trevor Gorven, who granted Booysen's application to have the murder and racketeering charges against him set aside and to declare Jiba's decision to prosecute him unconstitutional and invalid...

Justice Gorven was scathing about Jiba: 'I can conceive of no test for rationality, however relaxed, which could be satisfied by her explanation. The impugned decisions were arbitrary, offend the principle of legality and, therefore, the rule of law, and were unconstitutional.'

Although he'd been confident the state didn't have a case, Johan had consulted widely before taking on Jiba, acting head of the directorate of public prosecutions; Sello Maema, the lead prosecutor; Colonel Ncube, who had arrested him; National Police Commissioner Riah Phiyega; her deputy, Nobubele Mbekela; and KZN Police Commissioner Mmamonnye Ngobeni.

When I was first charged, my brother Marius had put me in touch with experienced silk Laurance Hodes, who agreed that racketeering charges would be almost impossible to prove. He had offered me a free consultation when I was next in Johannesburg. But, in the end, I employed the services of constitutional expert Anton Katz, from the Cape Bar.

To Johan's surprise, Laurance Hodes ended up acting for Jiba and co in opposing his application.

I thought it was unethical. If Hodes had told me that the state didn't have a case, why would he pretend to Jiba that there was one? Or mislead me?

Hodes says that at the time he spoke to Johan, he wasn't in a position to express a definite view of the merits of the matter. But he agreed to see him in Johannesburg 'to gain a better understanding'. He didn't hear from Johan again and he disclosed that he'd had a discussion with him to Jiba and her team.

Johan still thinks it was unethical.

Jiba hadn't attended court proceedings, but had objected, via Hodes, to the case being heard in Durban. Johan thought it an attempt to frustrate him. Advocate Hodes told the court that Jiba's decision to prosecute Booysen had been taken in Pretoria and the matter should be heard there. Katz argued that his client's constitutional rights had been affected in Durban. The judge agreed and the case was heard in Durban.

In court, Anton Katz SC called Jiba a liar: 'She is mendacious ... and took into account facts that did not exist ... she lied to this court.'

The court heard that Jiba had signed off on the decision to prosecute based on two statements from Aiyer and one from Danikas and Ndlondlo.

She'd said in her answering affidavit: 'there is prima facie evidence that an offence has been committed ... particular reference is made ... to the statements made by Colonel Ranjendran Aiyer, Mr Aris Danikas and Mr Ndlondlo from which it is apparent that the Applicant is well aware of the information.'

Johan *wasn't* well aware of the information because it hadn't been in the dockets given to him during the discovery process. Nor did he think that Jiba had ever planned to use the statements. From a source, he had obtained an email in which Jiba asked Advocate Anthony Mosing, who had assisted in the case, to explain to her why Johan had been charged.

Mosing gave her a vague answer. Jiba sent a follow-up email: 'My request was simply to make me understand the whole issue about the evidence that we had when the authorisation was issued ...'

She had, Johan assumed, rubber-stamped the application without reading the prosecution memorandum and had only later realised – or been told – that she didn't have enough evidence.

After my legal challenge, she must have asked the investigators for whatever they could come up with and was given the three statements, which didn't help at all: Ndlondlo was deceased, her own prosecutor Sello Maema had said Danikas' evidence shouldn't be used and Aiyer's was just office politics. When challenged, she said she'd 'applied her mind to the facts before her'.

Advocate Anton Katz told the court Jiba's decisions had been made irrationally and without relevant information.

Judge Trevor Gorven agreed that the charges didn't meet the barest of minimum requirements: 'Even accepting the least stringent test for rationality imaginable, the decision of the NDPP does not pass muster.'

Jiba, he wrote in his judgment, hadn't even tried to explain how she had reached her decision: 'In response to Mr Booysen's assertion of mendacity on her part, there is a deafening silence. In such circumstances, the court is entitled to draw an inference adverse to the NDPP.'

In March 2014, prosecutor Sello Maema asked the Durban High Court to withdraw the charges against Johan.

'All charges against you have been withdrawn. You are free to go,' the judge told him.

Round One: Booysen.

•

The battle lines had been drawn. Johan thought Jiba a dangerous person to have humiliated.

The court case had obviously cast aspersions on her character. From that moment on she seemed determined to get even. She had demonstrated the same vengeance against prosecutor Gerrie Nel, who had prosecuted her husband for fraud. Nel too had been arrested on a trumped-up charge.

Jiba has frequently said that the criticism levelled against her in various court judgments is unjustified and without bearing on her fitness for office.

But her powers had diminished. In 2013 she'd had to step down from her temporary leadership position and the NPA had a new head, Mxolisi Nxasana. At the time of Gorven's judgment, Nxasana had been overseas. Jiba, as his deputy, had instructed the state attorney to appeal. On his return, Nxasana had halted the process, because, he said, the case wasn't winnable.

Nxasana and Jiba did not share the same agendas. She blamed him for Danikas' statement not being signed. She had wanted to set up a mutual legal assistance agreement with authorities in Greece to get it signed, but Nxasana had interfered. In response to an application by the General Council of the Bar to have her struck from the roll of advocates for lying about evidence she had, or didn't have, against Booysen, she said: 'The Prosecutions team were confident that the statement would ultimately be signed ... however it remains unsigned as the prosecutions team, in particular Advocate Maema, was instructed by the current National Director of Public Prosecutions Mr Mxolisi Nxasana to halt the process.'

Jiba said that Danikas' statement was intended to corroborate the evidence in the possession of the prosecution team that 'Booysen was involved in the various activities giving rise to the charges against him as similar fact evidence, which is admissible in racketeering prosecutions'.

Johan didn't think she understood the concept of similar fact evidence in racketeering.

Even if what Danikas had said in his statement had been true it had nothing to do with racketeering. He said I'd laughed when he told me about Cato Manor shooting people in the street with pellet guns and that I had condoned torture; that I had once punched someone in front of him. What has this got to do with racketeering? If he'd said I had met regularly with Cato Manor and given them orders to kill people – that would be racketeering. But he didn't say that.

Charges withdrawn, Johan wanted to go back to work. But he was still suspended, as was Cato Manor.

> *According to police regulations we should have faced disciplinary proceedings within 60 days. It was coming up to 600 days since my suspension.*

The disciplinary hearing eventually got going in March 2014. Chairman Nazeer Cassim berated SAPS for delaying proceedings:

> In my ten years of experience chairing disciplinary enquiries, it is usually the employee that seeks delays and employs other technical defences to avoid the merits being ventilated. In this case, Booysen wanted his day in court sooner than later so that he could, from his perspective, return to field duty to do that which he knows best – police work – to make our society safer …

SAPS had spared no cost. Usually disciplinaries were conducted in-house. But for Johan, Deputy National Commissioner Nobubele Mbekela had hired senior counsel and two advocates to enable SAPS to 'deal with the matter sensibly and judiciously'. The first part of the hearing was held in Durban, then moved to Advocates' Chambers in Sandton and the latter part took place at the upmarket Beverley Hills Hotel in Umhlanga.

Johan and Carl van der Merwe would arrive at the hearing with a trolley case of papers. In comparison, they thought, the police witnesses floundered, quoted from incorrect interdicts and were unable to back up their case.

The chairman seemed to agree: 'No direct evidence was placed before me. The witnesses who testified on behalf of SAPS could not directly implicate Booysen in any wrongdoing.'

The SAPS main witness was a major general on the same level as Johan. His contribution was to testify about the proper conduct of a diligent commander, whom, he said, would have charged the Cato Manor officers after the Bongani Mkhize shooting.

Van der Merwe asked him why. Because, he said, they'd acted unlawfully.

Johan hauled out Police Minister Nathi Mthethwa's plea in the Mkhize civil case in which it was stated that Cato Manor had acted lawfully and that he, Mthethwa, was the SAPS commander in chief.

The major general conceded that Cato Manor couldn't have acted unlawfully. With their witness having fallen flat, SAPS scrambled around trying to find others to prove their case. Johan and Van der Merwe looked on bemused.

Instead of lasting a week or two, as disciplinary hearings should, proceedings dragged on for six months, while they tried to find witnesses.

Provincial Commissioner Ngobeni flatly refused to testify, which Chairman Cassim found perplexing: 'I would have expected Provincial Commissioner Ngobeni to come and give evidence before me to deal with these serious and damning allegations concerning her that not only discredit the SAPS ... but suggest corruption at the highest level.'

It was Colonel Subramoney that made the serious and damning allegations Cassim heard at the disciplinary hearing. He'd been Johan's trump card – and a wild card. He had first approached Hawks investigator, Van Loggerenberg, to testify in his defence. To Johan's dismay, the request was refused.

Colonel Van Loggerenberg was a detective who had worked on the Panday case, who could speak out for me and tell them that the case was directly linked to the PC's involvement in corruption. But he was told he couldn't. No one was allowed to help me. Or even talk to me.

Then Johan had located Subramoney – who had known the ins and outs of the case – and who had mysteriously disappeared, supposedly into the bowels of Crime Intelligence.

I traced him to Benoni, where he'd been twiddling his thumbs for three years after being lured away by Richard Mdluli. He agreed to testify. I told him not to breathe a word, or even to phone me in case they were monitoring my calls.

On the day he was to testify, Johan met Subramoney outside the Gautrain Station in Sandton and took him to the hearing. He had proceeded to blow SAPS' case to shreds. Subramoney told Chairman Cassim that Ngobeni, as well as Madhoe and Narainpershad were in a corrupt relationship with Panday, resulting in large sums of SAPS money being unaccounted for. He said Ngobeni had caused him to be 'orchestrated out of KZN' when the investigation was at an advanced stage, by getting Richard Mdluli to put the fear of God into him by telling him that if he had carried on with the Panday investigation his wife could end up without a husband, his children without a father.

At the end of Subramoney's evidence, Chairman Cassim had put down his pen and said: 'This is beginning to sound like a movie.'

It was at this point that SAPS' lead prosecutor asked for a remand. They hadn't banked on Subramoney's evidence. They would have to get Provincial Commissioner Ngobeni to respond.

Johan knew she wouldn't; they would make mincemeat of her.

He was right. Weeks passed – then, at the eleventh hour, National Police Commissioner Riah Phiyega arrived at the hearing, as if shielding Ngobeni. It infuriated Johan. He would later write to IPID:

The fact that General Ngobeni failed to testify in my hearing to rebut serious allegations regarding her interference in the corruption investigation was disquieting. If she was innocent she would've utilised the opportunity presented to her during my hearing to set the record straight. Instead General Phiyega arrived. In my 38 years of service I am not aware of a National Commissioner ever testifying in a disciplinary hearing.

Chairman Cassim's eyebrows were raised again: 'On the last day of the sitting, almost a month after serious allegations against the Provincial Commissioner of KwaZulu-Natal were made under oath with detailed amplification, and in rebuttal, not the Provincial Commissioner Ngobeni, but General Phiyega, the National Commissioner testified.'

Phiyega hadn't been part of SAPS when the Panday/Madhoe investigation began and, it seemed, hadn't bothered to get briefed. She told the hearing she was unaware that PC Ngobeni had tried to stop the Panday investigation.

Johan thought she was naive.

How could she possibly believe that the provincial commissioner and Panday had an innocuous relationship? How had Panday known the exact date of my suspension unless the PC had told him? And when Madhoe would return to work?

Chairman Cassim was equally unimpressed by Phiyega's evidence:

She had no insight or any knowledge of any details of the factual content relating to these events. She was sadly unable to deal with the state of play of senior police officers in particular, the Provincial Commissioner Ngobeni and Madhoe … I find this wholly unsatisfactory and it supports, if not augments the contention that the charges against Booysen were contrived to get rid of him.

It would be unjust not to forthwith reinstate Booysen to his position as provincial head of Priority Crime Investigation in KZN, so that he can do what he is best suited to do, that is to fight crime.

NAZEER CASSIM SC
Sandton Chambers
16 September 2014

Phiyega immediately applied to have the findings set aside. Johan wasn't surprised – the stakes were high – but he was disappointed in her.

She had impressed me when she had first started in the job. Although she knew nothing about policing, she had travelled the provinces getting ideas to improve things. She was articulate and, given the right support, I thought she would make it. But clearly she was taking advice from the wrong people – people with their own agendas – and didn't seem to give a damn about the cost to the taxpayer.

Phiyega would later explain her conduct, saying that she believed there would be 'chaos' if Booysen and Ngobeni worked in the same place.

Johan wrote to her that he would be opposing her application and that, by law, she had to send him a full record of the hearing. She sent it, but excluded the transcripts of her own evidence – which was dismal – and Subramoney's – which was damning.

I informed her that she was obliged to file the full record for the review to go ahead. It was obvious she was being selective because the transcripts of her own evidence would've compromised her and shown up Ngobeni's absence.

None was forthcoming, so he consulted Hawks head Anwa Dramat, who told him to go back to work, which he did on 22 September 2014.

My office chair was hardly warm when Dramat phoned and said Phiyega wanted to see me. I should go to Pretoria at my earliest convenience.

He and Dramat waited outside her office for five hours before she pitched.

When she arrived, dressed in police uniform, she said trust had broken down between me and General Ngobeni and gave me three options: I could apply for a transfer to another province, take early retirement and get paid out for the remainder of my contract, or go on 'special leave' while I contemplated my future. She gave me a month to decide. I didn't like any of her options and I certainly wasn't going to take early retirement, even though it would've meant getting paid out R2.5 million over and above my pension. To me it would be like taking a pay-off.

A month later Johan went back to Pretoria to give her his answer. This time she was only two hours late, dressed in civilian clothes and looking pleased with herself.

'So ... what have you decided?' She beamed at him and rubbed her hands together.

Johan told her he'd made up his mind and that he wasn't going anywhere.

I didn't see why I should go and work somewhere else because PC Ngobeni felt uncomfortable in my presence. I told her I wasn't going to stay on leave either – it was against regulations.

Her smile vanished in an instant.

'So if I give you an instruction to be relocated you will defy it?'

I will challenge it.

'On what basis?'

In terms of the amendment to the Police Act, which says that you cannot transfer me.

The Hawks fell under the DPCI – the Directorate of Priority Crime Investigation. It was Dramat's job to take action against him, not Phiyega's.

She looked down at Dramat, over whom she towered.

'What do you say?'

'I agree with the general.'

She asked Johan to leave and told Dramat she needed to talk to him. As he got up and left, Johan told her he would be back in his office on duty the following day.

After an hour, Dramat joined me and we went for coffee. He said Phiyega had asked him what made me tick. He told her that I wanted to get on with my job and that there was nothing to stop me.

Over coffee, he and Dramat decided that, in the interests of good working relationships, he would, despite the fact that he'd already been on suspension for close on two years, take vacational leave then meet with Ngobeni and Phiyega to clear the air. They had two weeks to reconsider their position.

The meeting, a fortnight later, didn't serve to do that at all. Johan says Ngobeni launched into him.

She said I had humiliated and undermined her and leaked negative stories about her to newspapers. She accused me of plotting against her with Bheki Cele and of being involved with drug lords.

Then she started crying. Loudly. Johan was unimpressed.

Deputy National Commissioner Mbekela went to fetch tissues and started rubbing her back as if to soothe her. I felt nothing – she'd made my life very difficult. I told her she couldn't deny that she'd stopped the Panday investigation.

That made her sob even louder, saying Johan was against her: 'I don't know if it's because I am a woman or because I don't have straight hair!'

Johan rolled his eyes and glanced at Dramat – normally a placid person. He looked completely fed up.

Johan addressed Phiyega.

I told her it was my constitutional obligation to investigate corruption and if Ngobeni didn't trust me, perhaps it had something to do with her own conduct. Then I left.

Phiyega still hadn't provided a transcript of her evidence for the review of his disciplinary finding, so Johan went back to work. Most people seemed happy to see him.

•

In the following weeks he kept away from Ngobeni, never seeking her out, but greeting her politely if he happened to cross her path.

One of the colonels who dealt with her told me that she frequently asked if I was at work and what I was doing.

One day Johan got into the lift and there was Colonel Navin Madhoe, back in his old job at Supply Chain Management.

'Morning, general!' Madhoe said cheerfully.

'I don't know how you sleep at night,' Johan muttered under his breath.

It made me more determined to reinstate charges against him. Cato Manor was still facing racketeering charges with no evidence, but with piles of files against Madhoe and Panday, KZN public prosecution's head Moipone Noko had withdrawn charges against them. She'd sat with the docket for two years and refused to return it to investigators. She had also declined to prosecute Ngobeni for benefiting from Panday.

In October 2014 Noko had decided there wasn't a case against Panday and Madhoe, stating: 'Case 781 [the World Cup fraud] was dealt with by the SCCU in Durban and disposed of recently with a decision not to prosecute anyone as there was no evidence to prosecute any person with any offence.'

In making her decision Noko seemed to have relied on a prosecutor at the Specialised Commercial Crime Unit, Abram Letsholo. He'd accepted Panday's version of events as true and said that the monitoring of his electronic communications was proof of 'agendas among parties and scores to settle': 'Mr Panday and Colonel Madhoe were being pressurised to falsely implicate the provincial commissioner in the commission of criminal offences, with a promise that they will be exonerated in 781 [the World Cup fraud].'

Noko decided she believed Panday; she believed Johan was gunning for the PC's job. Johan wrote to her boss, NDPP head Mxolisi Nxasana, and to his boss, Anwa Dramat. This is what he alleged:

That they believe the suspect's version over the police version raises to my mind a question of serious impropriety ... It is common cause that Panday's calls were intercepted ... even if they would argue that the calls are inadmissible as evidence, it does not render them illegal.

Noko demonstrated her ignorance of the evidence at her disposal ... I had never applied for the job as provincial commissioner ... the investigation in any event focused on irregularities before the provincial commissioner assumed the post. She attempted to interfere with the investigation after she assumed her position ...

Noko seemed not to have read the statements at all. She thought that the suspended Cato Manor Unit had conducted the Panday investigation, saying the objectivity of the detectives was questionable as they had a cloud hanging over their heads.

Johan was amazed that, despite having had the docket for two years, Noko hadn't yet got her head around it. He told Nxasana:

None of these investigating officers was ever attached to the Cato Manor Unit. They are not implicated in the Cato Manor issue at all.

Noko seemed unaware that Ngobeni's own finance department had initiated the investigation. Her apparent lack of background information astonished Johan.

Had Advocate Noko bothered to examine Brigadier Kemp's statement, she would have established the source of this entire investigation. There is a prima facie case against Mr Thoshan Panday, Colonel Navin Madhoe, as well as Captain Aswin Narainpershad. The evidence is contained in 20 lever-arch files, more than 200 affidavits, as well as a forensic auditor report by PricewaterhouseCoopers.

•

Johan was in his office on 11 December 2014 when he received a call to say there was encrypted email for him. He needed a code to access it. Strange, Johan thought. He phoned Dramat's PA in Pretoria who gave him the code. It was from Phiyega, saying he should give her reasons why he shouldn't be dismissed from the police.

She said the trust relationship had broken down between him and his provincial commissioner.

Johan thought he knew exactly what she was up to, trying to get rid of him just before Christmas so he couldn't seek relief because the courts would be in recess.

I wrote back, giving Phiyega three days to withdraw the letter or else I would get an interdict to prevent her dismissing me. She didn't, so I got an interdict. It was probably the first time in South African history that a general had obtained an interdict against the national commissioner.

Dramat suggested Johan contact police watchdog IPID, whose job it was to investigate wrongdoing at SAPS. Johan was hesitant. He had reservations about IPID Executive Director, Robert McBride.

McBride had always been persona non grata to me. I thought he was probably a political appointment. But a lecturer I knew told me that he'd done a degree in policing and was an astute student. Still I had reservations, until I had a call from him in late 2014, asking for a written report on Commissioner Ngobeni. There had been a complaint in parliament and he was acting on it.

He wrote to McBride about Phiyega: 'General Phiyega does not utilise the disciplinary regulations in the spirit for which they are intended. She abuses the regulations to persecute certain individuals in order to protect others.'

Johan cited the example of Colonel Aiyer. A magistrate had ordered that Aiyer be investigated for contaminating a crime scene and defeating the course of justice, yet no disciplinary charges had ever been put to him. And he mentioned Western Cape Provincial Commissioner General Arno Lamoer, whom Phiyega had tipped off about a Hawks investigation into Lamoer's alleged involvement with crime syndicates.

'General Phiyega,' he wrote, 'had an obligation in terms of police regulations to initiate disciplinary steps. As a primary custodian of the Constitution she is obliged to exercise her mandate in a fair and equitable manner. She has, however, demonstrated the converse.'

Something else that Phiyega had done was to demand the recordings of Panday's intercepted phone calls. These were in the possession of Colonel Brian Padayachee, from KZN Crime Intelligence. She knew about them because Padayachee had written to her and to Dramat, saying: 'The intercepts revealed very sensitive information implicating high-profile individuals who have had a corrupt relationship with Mr Panday. Payment for favours was evident.'

In an affidavit, Padayachee had stated: 'The intercepts further revealed how Mr Panday was assisted by several police officials in obtaining crime scene photographs to conspire against Major General Booysen. These very photographs were subsequently leaked to the media and published in the *Sunday Times*, which eventually led to the criminal charges and suspension of Major General Booysen.'

Padayachee was suspended for his efforts, after 33 years in the police. He wrote to Phiyega: 'I sought your guidance and assistance with this investigation but instead departmental action has been initiated against me.'

•

Johan wrote his report to Robert McBride on a Saturday.

By the Sunday he had read it and had responded. Within a week he had sent investigators to KZN. He gets things done. Normally when police officials from out of town have work to do in Durban they book into hotels and take as long as possible at state expense. Not at IPID under McBride. I was impressed. Like me, he's a bit of a slave driver.

After the preliminary report had been written, McBride flew to Durban to discuss the case with Johan. They might have once differed ideologically, but now they had a common purpose. Johan began respecting him.

He's intelligent and grasped the dynamics of the case. I can be a bit forceful, I know, but he doesn't force his ideas and doesn't pretend to know everything. All my negative feelings towards him dissipated. What struck me about him is that he doesn't give up. He told me he would pursue the matter and he did.

McBride arranged a meeting for Johan with prosecutor Gerrie Nel, auditors PricewaterhouseCoopers and a team from IPID. Johan and the PWC forensic auditor presented to them the facts of the Panday/Ngobeni case.

At the end Gerrie Nel said, 'So what's the problem – why can't you prosecute?' He said it was clear cut: we should first pursue the R2-million attempted bribery case and then the R15-million corruption case involving Panday, but that we should redo the phone transcripts between him and Kevin Stephen – they weren't clear enough – so IPID had them redone, word for word. What came up on the intercept transcripts the second time round was that Panday and Madhoe had something on Stephen and were threatening to reveal all unless he got the documentation Panday wanted.

In the meantime, McBride had written and personally delivered a letter to Police Minister Nathi Nhleko, who in May that year, 2014, had replaced Nathi Mthethwa. McBride recommended that Phiyega be suspended to allow IPID to investigate her.

'Watch,' he said to Johan, 'I'll be next.'

Never, thought Johan. Surely McBride was one of the untouchables.

McBride told Nhleko that Phiyega had 'interfered in the investigation of alleged corruption by suspending Booysen, a key witness in the corruption and bribery cases', and 'instead of disciplining Ngobeni for failure to report and investigate allegations of corruption, she'd initiated disciplinary action against Booysen'.

McBride accused Phiyega of ignoring provisions of the Protected Disclosures Act by testifying on Ngobeni's behalf during Booysen's disciplinary hearing where 'serious allegations were made' against Ngobeni.

'According to the findings made by the chairperson in the disciplinary proceedings against Booysen, the National Commissioner interfered in the disciplinary proceedings by testifying about incidents she knew nothing about.'

McBride sent IPID investigators to question Ngobeni, which got her into a flat spin. She found herself a lawyer, the same one used by Madhoe and Panday. Johan wondered if Panday had paid for it.

Ngobeni went on the offensive:

DAILY NEWS
23 DECEMBER 2014
'THEY WANT TO OUST ME'

'I have been investigated three times about my husband's party matter, and nothing was found against me. I'm disappointed with the way people would try everything to get what they want ... I have a certificate from the public prosecutor indicating that the prosecutor declined to prosecute because there was no case against me, but individuals with ulterior motives continue to pursue the matter.'

Panday joined in and took a swipe at the media for 'haunting' Ngobeni: 'Why can't you leave a black woman in power to do her job? Why don't you haunt the white men in high positions?'

At the NPA, Mxolisi Nxasana ordered a review of the Noko decision to drop charges against Panday, Madhoe, Narainpershad and Ngobeni and gave the docket to Gerrie Nel. Nxasana also launched an internal investigation into his deputy, Nomgcobo Jiba. Senior counsel recommended to him that she be criminally investigated for perjury and fraud. According to counsel, there was reasonable suspicion that she had lied under oath about the evidence she had against Johan.

For the first time in months, Johan was upbeat. He had allies where it mattered – albeit unlikely ones, as the *Mail & Guardian*'s Sam Sole pointed out in an analysis piece headlined 'Jacob Zuma and the untouchable Mr Panday', suggesting that 'one man and his relationship with the Zuma family' were central to the 'havoc in the criminal justice system'. Sole summed up the players: 'Booysen, the hard-nosed white career cop; McBride, the Wentworth wide boy turned Umkhonto weSizwe soldier… now stubborn watchman over police abuse; Dramat, the loyal, quiet Cape activist turned corruption-buster; and Nxasana, the small-time Durban lawyer elevated to the pinnacle of the prosecution service.'

But the alliance was about to come crashing down.

Two days before Christmas 2014, Hawks head Anwa Dramat was suspended. McBride would soon follow.

- 18 -

ROLLMOPS AND CORRUPTION BUSTERS

In March 2015 Johan was invited to an anti-corruption conference in Gauteng. He'd been to a few of them in the past ten years.

Each seemed to be a rehash of the last and another reminder that corruption could be combated if laws were properly enforced.

This one, organised by the Justice cluster and held at Emperor's Palace on the East Rand, was called 'The Serious Corruption Conference' – focusing on graft involving government officials and over R5 million.

Johan was interested in who would be attending. The new acting head of the Hawks, Berning Ntlemeza, who'd begun his career in the former Transkei and who had previously served as deputy police commissioner in Limpopo, would be there. Anwa Dramat was suspended, ostensibly because of the unlawful deportation of Zimbabwean suspects.

Ntlemeza had weighed in and suspended Gauteng Hawks head Shadrack Sibiya for the same alleged offence. They were archrivals: Ntlemeza, a Richard Mdluli ally, had accused Sibiya of plotting against him, stating in an intelligence report in 2009: 'It is clear that there was a plot within the crime intelligence environment to prevent divisional commissioner Mdluli ... from being appointed as the head of crime intelligence of the South African Police Service.'

When Sibiya challenged his suspension in court, Ntlemeza testified that Sibiya had threatened subordinates and that an officer who had implicated him in the illegal renditions had 'mysteriously died'. But on 23 March 2015 Judge Elias Matojane found that Ntlemeza's decision to suspend Sibiya was unlawful and invalid – and that Ntlemeza was untruthful. The officer had died of natural causes: 'I am of the view that the conduct of the third respondent shows that he is biased and dishonest. To show that the third respondent is biased, lacks integrity and honour, he made false statements under oath.'

Dramat, who had been cleared by IPID of the rendition allegations, believed his own suspension was linked to investigations he was taking on. He had, two days prior to his suspension, called for the Nkandla docket from the detective services.

On Christmas Eve 2014 Dramat had written to Police Minister Nathi Nhleko: 'No doubt you are aware that I have recently called for certain case dockets involving very influential persons to be brought or alternatively centralised under one investigating arm and this has clearly caused massive resentment towards me.'

Johan thought that Dramat's support for him against Riah Phiyega couldn't have helped either.

IPID's Robert McBride, who had cleared both Dramat and Sibiya, stepped into the fray and told the police minister that his appointment of Ntlemeza as acting head of the Hawks was political interference; the Constitutional Court had ruled that only parliament could fire the head of the Hawks.

McBride was suspended, too, and in 2016 would be charged with fraud for allegedly altering a report in order to exonerate Dramat. McBride claimed in court papers that he had been a victim of a conspiracy; Ntlemeza and Richard Mdluli, he said, had conspired to oust Dramat.

When Ntlemeza addressed 'The Serious Corruption Conference', he told delegates, in what seemed to Johan to be a vitriolic tirade, that he had the right to request any docket and nobody could question him. This was in apparent reference to his attempts to get hold of the Jiba perjury and fraud docket, which prosecutors were refusing to give him.

The delegates to the conference were high level, from all over the country. Ntlemeza appeared to have no sense of occasion; he acted like a commander in chief addressing a bunch of troops. Several people thought he was completely out of order.

Johan hoped the Police and Justice ministers would realise what a buffoon Ntlemeza was before the time came to make a permanent appointment.

Or perhaps that's precisely why they would appoint him. It was a scary thought.

Ntlemeza went on, stating the obvious: corruption cases should be identified early to try to improve the quality and turnaround time of investigations. That's exactly what he had tried to do, Johan thought. He had acted on Brigadier Kemp's suspicions of corruption involving Panday and Supply Chain Management as soon as he'd heard about it.

And where did it get me? Suspended twice, in court thrice and accused of murder and racketeering. I looked around the room and saw the connected cabal that had gone out of its way to block me: Nomgcobo Jiba, accused of lying about the evidence she had against me and facing perjury charges; Lawrence Mrwebi, who had dropped corruption charges against Richard Mdluli and urged prosecutors to do the same with Panday; Sello Maema, the lead prosecutor in the Cato Manor case who had falsely intimated that Ndlondlo had been killed; and Raymond Mathenjwa, the state prosecutor who'd had no compassion for Shane Naidoo in court after his brother had died, nor for Neville Eva, dying from organ failure. Instead he had said they should be in leg irons.

That was three years ago. Neville Eva was dead, so was Vincent Auerbach; Willie Oliver had retired but the rest of the accused, 26 of them, were still suspended on full pay. Despite the hullaballoo and the headlines, the case had gone nowhere. Each time they appeared in court, it was postponed again. They hadn't yet even had their SAPS disciplinary. Ironically, at court appearances they would be handed their payslips.

At lunch at the conference, Johan was serving himself some rollmops when he became aware of Jiba next to him. He had never met her before.

He dipped his head and passed her the tongs. She said a curt 'Thank you'. He watched her walk back to her table.

When she got there she said something to Mathenjwa whom she was sitting next to. He looked up, saw me and hastily looked away. Clearly my presence made them uncomfortable. Their attempts to prosecute me had blown up in their faces.

He walked over to Advocate Mathenjwa and tapped him on the shoulder. He shook Johan's hand and said: 'Ooh, if the media could see us now.' A few people laughed and Maema said they should take a photograph. Johan thought of a few choice captions for it.

On day two, Lawrence Mrwebi, so often accused of being at the forefront of irrational decisions and power struggles within the NPA, addressed the conference. He said, inappropriately, Johan thought, that he wasn't afraid of Richard Mdluli.

He must've been referring to Judge John Murphy's finding, after an application by legal lobby group Freedom Under Law, that Mrwebi's decision to drop charges against Mdluli was 'illegal, irrational, based on irrelevant considerations and material errors of law, and ultimately so unreasonable that no reasonable prosecutor could have taken it'.

Justice Murphy hadn't held back when it came to Jiba either, saying that her and Mrwebi's conduct signalled 'a troubling lack of appreciation of the constitutional ethos and principles underpinning the offices they held'. They did not, he said, demonstrate that they had the capacity to pursue matters without fear or favour.

Now Mrwebi, charged with defeating the ends of justice by the NPA for instructing prosecutor Glynnis Breytenbach to provisionally withdraw fraud and corruption charges against Richard Mdluli, was standing there imploring prosecutors only to prosecute if they had prima facie evidence. The same Mrwebi, thought Johan, who seemed unable to recognise evidence unless it suited his agenda and who had tried to convince a prosecutor to withdraw charges against Panday because 'all' Johan had had was 'an ATM slip'.

The wisest words of the conference as far as Johan was concerned came from Chief Justice Mogoeng Mogoeng. He spoke movingly about his visit to the graves of liberation heroes Moses Kotane and JB Marks in Moscow and how he had been overcome with sadness thinking about what they had died for. He said he was sorry South Africa had the need for an anti-corruption conference at all and that some of those who publicly opposed corruption were often the biggest perpetrators. What was needed was a collective resolve to fight it: 'Do so irrespective of who is involved, how powerful he or she is or how connected ...'

Johan made a point of nodding vehemently in agreement, glancing over at the cabal and clapping loudly after everyone else had stopped.

On the last day Nomgcobo Jiba, under investigation for fraud and perjury after the Gorven Judgement in Johan's favour, said prosecutors should make sure there was evidence before making decisions. Perhaps she had learned from experience, he thought. It might, of course, have been a subtle jab at whoever at the NPA would be dealing with her case.

That would be Senior Deputy Director of Public Prosecutions Jan Ferreira. He was at the conference too. He and State Advocate Gerhard van Eeden had drawn up a memo for the NDPP, saying that the evidence against Booysen had been seriously flawed. The decision to prosecute Jiba, by contrast, was 'sound in law and in line with the NPA Act', according to their memo:

> In ten of the murder cases against Booysen and Cato Manor, primer residue had been found on the hands of 10 of the alleged victims ... It is uncertain how the prosecution team ... intends to get past the evidence that primer residue was found on the hands of the deceased ... unless they possess evidence that this ... was manipulated ... we have not seen any such evidence ...

•

Not long after the conference, on 24 March 2015, a summons was issued to serve on Jiba. But the investigating officer, Colonel Boats Botha, couldn't find her – she wasn't at home, she wasn't at work. So the summons for her to appear in court on 21 April on charges of fraud and perjury was served on her boss, Mxolisi Nxasana.

What happened next was an indication of the extent of the rift between the police, under Riah Phiyega, and the NPA. Phiyega took Boats Botha off the case and had him replaced; he was accused of secretly colluding with the NPA against Jiba. Phiyega's spokesman Solomon Makgale went on radio and insisted that SAPS wasn't looking for her:

'It is our view that the NPA, who are also complainants in the matter, jumped the gun when they issued a summons against Advocate Jiba.'

Makgale told Talk Radio 702 that the investigating officer, Major General Norman Taioe, hadn't been consulted by the NPA. What he didn't say was that this was because Taioe was brand new. Phiyega had terminated Boats Botha's contract and, according to the *Mail & Guardian* on 27 March 2015, had phoned Nxasana, frantically insisting that the process was flawed and that the person who presented himself as the investigating officer was not the investigating officer. Therefore Jiba's summons wasn't valid, she'd told him.

The *Mail & Guardian*'s Qaanitah Hunter wrote in an article entitled: '"Fugitive' Jiba face to face with NPA boss' that Nxasana was fuming. 'I have a problem now because they are questioning my integrity ... they are saying I lied,' he said. 'The problem is my integrity and the integrity of the organisation [the NPA] is at stake.

'I have reason to believe that the national police commissioner was interfering in the case,' he alleged. 'And this was not the first time. It has happened before.'

And so began a very public spat between Phiyega and Nxasana:

EYEWITNESS NEWS
27 MARCH 2015
NXASANA: PUBLIC PERCEPTION OF JIBA IS DISTURBING
BY BARRY BATEMAN AND MANDY WIENER

JOHANNESBURG – National Director of Public Prosecutions Mxolisi Nxasana ... said the intervention of National Commissioner Riah Phiyega in the Jiba matter was worrying.

'I asked her and I'm asking the same question. Does she really do this to all other matters, where other ordinary suspects are involved? That is my concern.'

Pikkie Greeff, in the *Daily Maverick* on 2 April 2015, marvelled at Jiba's extraordinary influence or connections that enabled her:

To get the entire SAPS management involved in a quick replacement of an investigating officer with the specific purpose of creating an, albeit flawed, legal gap for invalidating an issued summons ... Even to such an extent that the Commissioner would venture well outside her jurisdiction and confront the kingpin lawyer at the NPA on what is essentially a legal argument. The question is: how much clout must one actually have to get authorities right at the top level to dive into a half-assed rescue plan?

Jiba had been criticised by judges in three different courts, accused of lying, failing to comply with court orders, ignoring deadlines, failing to exercise an independent mind, and 'shielding irrational and illegal actions from judicial scrutiny'.

Nxasana recommended to President Zuma that an inquiry be held into Jiba's conduct. But when President Zuma finally announced in February 2015 that an inquiry into the NPA would be established it wasn't Jiba he targeted. Instead, it was Nxasana's fitness for office that should be probed.

Nazeer Cassim was appointed as presiding officer. But at the eleventh hour, the inquiry was cancelled. Johan had been looking forward to seeing what Cassim would make of Zuma's attempts to get rid of Nxasana.

Cassim had ruled in my favour at my disciplinary hearing and had been very critical of Riah Phiyega and SAPS – he wasn't one to mince his words. Had the NPA inquiry gone ahead, he could very likely have swept aside the president's assertion that Nxasana wasn't fit for office. Had Cassim decided that Nxasana was fit for office, this would have given Nxasana the authority to act against Jiba, Mrwebi, Ngobeni, Panday and the rest of the cabal.

Instead the president said he would 'engage' with Nxasana. The result of the engagement was a hefty R17-million payout and a new chief prosecutor for South Africa.

At a press conference on 18 August 2015, new NDPP Shaun Abrahams announced that all charges against Jiba would be dropped: 'There has been no finding by a court that Advocate Jiba has acted dishonestly ... my experience in working with her is that she performs her duties in an exemplary fashion.'

A week before this announcement, Johan had been told he was to be suspended again.

- 19 -

SUSPENDED AGAIN

The next offensive arrived on 11 August 2015, just days before Johan's interview for the post of national head of the Directorate for Priority Crime Investigation – the Hawks.

Anwa Dramat's old job was up for grabs, so Johan had applied. Why not, he thought – he was better qualified than most. He'd been a general in the Hawks for five years. Berning Ntlemeza was currently acting in the position. But now, although the racketeering charges against Johan had been withdrawn, Ntlemeza had sent him a 'notice of contemplated suspension' – for fraud.

Ntlemeza and the cabal seemed determined to find something to keep me suspended until I retired. This time the imputation was that I had fraudulently received a monetary award from SAPS and that I had supplied false case numbers to obtain the award.

Cato Manor and Johan had qualified for the awards after the Chonco case. In SAPS-speak they were 'a certificate of commendation from the National Commissioner coupled with a monetary award of R10 000'. They were the same awards that had been included in their racketeering indictments, as evidence that Cato Manor had killed for money.

Willie Olivier had done the paperwork and included Johan's name because he had tipped them off about Magojela Ndimande's whereabouts, which had led to the subsequent shooting in Howick. But Olivier had written a digit wrong in the case number and had put 08 instead of 09. It was clearly a typo – 09 referred to September – the date of the Howick shooting.

The 08 number was for a case of theft from a motor vehicle. Ntlemeza said this was evidence of fraud. Except he made a mistake too and said it was a housebreaking case.

On the standard-format document that Olivier had filled in was place for Johan's signature. But Johan hadn't signed it.

Because I stood to benefit I had deleted my name from the signature section and sent it to my immediate manager, Pat Brown. Brown signed it and sent it on to Commissioner Ngidi, who'd then referred it to the national office. Seven years later Ntlemeza hauled it out of the Cato Manor case file to use against me.

Ntlemeza said Johan and officers under his command had accepted money fraudulently, causing SAPS to suffer 'financially and reputationally'.

Proof of this, he said, was the document signed off by Olivier and Brown in which 08 had been written instead of 09.

A High Court judge would later find: 'This is not the kind of error likely to mislead even a junior police official.'

Ntlemeza had given Johan 24 hours to respond and say why he shouldn't be suspended.

I needed more time, so I phoned Ntlemeza; sent him a text message; emailed his work and private addresses. I knew he was avoiding me.

So Johan got stuck into his own response:

'I reject your imputation of impropriety by myself. It is an unlawful attack on my dignity, as well as defamatory.'

Ntlemeza had accused Johan and Cato Manor of claiming for monetary awards before the completion of the investigation into Chonco's death and said that those killed had not been suspects. Johan took exception:

'The assertion that none of the deceased was sought for Colonel Chonco's murder is misplaced. During an inquest held in 2010, the Magistrate at Maphumulo Magistrate's Court ruled that the following persons were *responsible ... Lindelani Buthelezi, Khopha Ntuli ...'*

He listed the names of suspects implicated in Chonco's death, all of whom had been shot by Cato Manor and for which Olivier had recommended awards. He detailed the chain of command in approving them: a provincial commissioner and two deputy national commissioners.

'Yet I am being singled out by you. This leaves me with the inescapable conclusion that I am being targeted for reasons best known to you.'

He asked why, after having been investigated by the Hawks and IPID, who were assisted by six prosecutors, no one had ever concluded he'd committed fraud, until now?

'... I was never charged for fraud in this regard. This also raises another question, as to whom "has recently" brought the so-called misrepresentation, as stated in your notice, to your attention? The only explanation I can conceive of is that it comes from Major General Mabula or someone from his team. They have had the disputed documents in their possession since 2012.'

Johan had found out that Ntlemeza's office had, three weeks before, asked Major General Brown for a statement about the awards. Brown had confirmed that he'd also recommended the payments, not Johan. So why, Johan responded to Ntlemeza, if he'd known this, did he proceed with the suspension? There could only be one reason.

'It is clear there is a male fide *agenda to neutralise me from continuing certain investigations and other processes currently underway in the DPCI. Should you proceed with the process, I shall apply for urgent relief from the court.'*

Johan drove to Pretoria to deliver his response to Ntlemeza personally.
A few days later he flew to Cape Town for his interview for the Hawks top job.

I wondered if the timing of the latest fraud charges had been a deliberate ploy by Ntlemeza to cast further aspersions on me in the week that I was to be interviewed for the highest post in the Directorate of Priority Crime Investigation.

The interview, on 18 August, was at the office of Minister of Police Nathi Nhleko. Johan arrived first. Three others arrived – one of them was Jan Mabula. Johan had recently instituted a civil claim against him.

I had demanded R10.8-million compensation from Mabula, Minister Nhleko, IPID's Glen Angus, who had assisted in my arrest, and Jiba, accusing them of wrongful arrest, malicious prosecution and abusing state institutions. I felt that they had continuously harassed me since I began the corruption investigation in 2011.

Now I had to sit in the same room as Mabula. It was an uncomfortable situation. I didn't bother to make small talk – I closed my eyes and dozed off until it was my turn to be interviewed.

During the interview with Nathi Nhleko, Justice Minister Michael Masutha, State Security Minister David Mahlobo and Deputy Police Minister Maggie Sotyu Johan was asked about the latest intended suspension.

I explained there was no evidence to suggest I was party to fraud to obtain awards for myself and Cato Manor.

He didn't get the job.

Berning Ntlemeza, who'd been acting in the Hawks post for seven months and who wasn't present on the day of the interviews, was appointed permanently on 10 September 2015. A competency check, said the interviewing committee, 'was deemed superfluous to the experience and track record of the preferred candidate'.

One of the first things the preferred candidate did in his new position was to gather an entourage to fly to Durban to suspend Johan. It was, Johan thought, an attempt by Ntlemeza and the minister of police to show Ngobeni where their allegiances lay.

But someone from HQ in Pretoria gave Johan the heads up and instead of going to the office he went to see a Crime Intelligence contact in Pietermaritzburg.

At about midday he started getting text messages from colleagues:

about how put out Ngobeni had been when she'd led Ntlemeza and armed members of the Tactical Response team to Johan's office, only to find it locked. She had demanded the key from his PA Elaine, who didn't have it. She and Ntlemeza had told Elaine if she didn't open the door she would be suspended too.

I knew it was just a way to try to intimidate me. They had no right to search my office. PC Ngobeni had been trying to intimidate me for five years, from when she first allowed Thoshan Panday to confront me in her office, to when she had got Phiyega to try to bully me.

Ntlemeza had called all the KZN Hawks detectives together and told them they weren't allowed to communicate with their now former commander. That included Johan's brother, Anton, a lieutenant colonel with Organised Crime.

So I couldn't speak to my own brother, even about personal stuff. They were trying to excommunicate me and make other people afraid. It was all so ridiculous so I decided to lay charges of my own against Ntlemeza for impairing my dignity. And for making misrepresentations. The notice of intention to suspend was in itself a fraudulent document.

Johan went back to his office late that afternoon after everyone had left. He wrote a statement saying that the allegations Ntlemeza had made in the suspension letter were wrong.

He'd said that the cases we'd claimed for weren't linked to the Chonco killing and that everything in the document was false. Even though there'd been inquests in some of these cases and a magistrate had ruled on them.

Then I went to the Durban Central police station and laid charges of crimen injuria and fraud against him. The captain at the charge office was surprised to see me – it wasn't often that a general came in to lay a complaint. He arranged with the provincial head of IPID to collect the docket.

That night Johan was contacted by an unlikely source, from deep within the corridors of power, and told to watch his back. He should sleep away from home and change his cellphone number. So he got a new sim card – for what it was worth – packed a bag, fed his bull terrier, Belize, and hit the road.

The following day he sat at Europa Café on Florida Road, taking call after call, from journalists, colleagues and lawyers. In the corner of the coffee shop, back to the wall, was a bodyguard in a black suit. At his feet a big bag containing an LM6 assault rifle. He also had a 9mm on him. It was a point at which most people would've thrown in the towel.

I'm gatvol, I admit it, but if I start something I must finish it. I can't capitulate. It's not in my nature. I'm not going to accept money as if I have done something wrong. I refused Phiyega's offer of a package, now suddenly I'm accused of fraud for a typing mistake made by someone else seven years ago and I am suspended again.

His daughter, Natalie, had wanted him to take the package, which would have amounted to R2.5 million, over and above a pension, after 38 years in the force. It upset her every time he got up, bloodied and bruised, to fight another round:

> He's always been Mr Fix-it, able to sort anything out. There have been so many attempts to get rid of him, sometimes it's hard to keep track and any normal person would've cracked up. It affects our whole family – sometimes we feel helpless. I have Google alerts on my phone – and when 'Booysen' pops up I think – oh no, what now?

His son Eben sent him a text message after the latest suspension: *'Ek weet nie of ek as seun van 'n pa of as suid afrikaner die meeste teleurgesteld is nie ... nie in dedda, maar in die mense wat die besluit gemaak het.'* ('I don't know if I'm more disappointed as a South African, or as your son, not in you Dad, but in the people that took this decision.')

Johan replied: *'Dis die lewe, seun. Ek vat dit op die ken en gaan aan.'* ('That's life, son. I take it on the chin and carry on.')

•

Johan walked across Florida Road to a computer shop.
 The bodyguard waited outside.
 Three men walked in.
 One of them was Schabir Shaik.
 The same Schabir Shaik who Aiyer had told everyone Johan wanted

to have killed.

Shaik stopped in front of him.

'Booysen!'

Johan looked up.

'You have my support. But you should have taken what Phiyega offered you. Never trust them. Fuck them! Fight them!'

- 20 -

ROUND SEVEN

In 2015 a question was put to parliament: the total cost to date for litigation against Major General Johan Booysen?

INTERNAL QUESTION PAPER NO 51-2015 4241
Mr ZN Mbhele (DA) to ask the Minister of Police:
What has been the total cost to date for litigation in all legal actions instituted against a certain person (name and details furnished) by the SA Police Service?
REPLY:
The total costs incurred to date amounts to R1 717 351-52 calculated as follows:
Disciplinary hearing R1 088 193-54
Review of the disciplinary hearing (SAPS) R226 062-00
Review of the arbitration (Maj Gen Booysen) R403 095-98
TOTAL R1 717 351-52

The answer of R1.7 million supplied by SAPS, says Johan, was incorrect and misleading.

That was just the cost of the failed disciplinary hearing, which Riah Phiyega had dragged out over six months. The amount was far greater: in four years I had taken on the office of the NDPP and SAPS six times, each time winning with costs. For each court appearance the state used senior counsel and so did I. And each time the taxpayer had to pay my costs too.

In November 2015 Judge Anton van Zyl found that there wasn't a 'shred of evidence' to support the fraud case against Johan, and that Hawks boss Berning Ntlemeza had relied on 'opinion, unsubstantiated by facts'.

Johan asked the judge for a cost order *de bonis propriis* – out of one's own pocket.

I wanted to force Ntlemeza to pay litigation costs from his own pocket, instead of the taxpayers. It was unfair that public money should be used to fund vexatious officials getting hammered in court – and then they would appeal – and use some more. Why should officials get away with wasting public money?

The cost order wasn't granted, but Van Zyl said Ntlemeza's conduct deserved censure and that the state should pay: 'As a mark of the court's disapproval I consider that costs on the scale between attorney and client would be justified.'

The advocate acting for the Hawks, William Mokhari, appeared to accept the decision and Johan went back to work. But when he arrived at his office, he couldn't get in. The locks had been changed. This, he was told, was 'procedural'.

Johan forced his way in – but not for long. His acting replacement, Major General Alfred Khana, arrived half an hour later to tell him Ntlemeza would be applying for leave to appeal the judgment. Johan doubted he had even read it.

He couldn't have, in less than an hour. But Ntlemeza didn't seem to care if the appeal failed or not, because on 1 January 2016, he appointed someone permanently in my position.

Major General Jabulani Zikhali had previously worked at Organised Crime's policy and standards section, a far cry from provincial head of the Hawks.

Johan had been running a slick operation when he was suspended for the first time in 2012, only to see working structures and systems dismantled by his replacements. A monitoring group set up to police chemicals used in drug manufacturing was closed down. An endangered species group met the same fate.

One of the things Zikhali did in his new position was to call the KZN Hawks together, tell them he was tired of innuendo and gossip and that Johan's professional legacy should be maintained. But Johan was expecting to get his job back.

I had no gripe with Zikhali, who was efficient and likeable. But I was interested in finding out what role I'd be playing within the KZN Hawks should Ntlemeza be refused leave to appeal.

I phoned Zikhali, congratulated him under the circumstances and briefed him about a corruption case I'd been tipped off about, involving the private sector.

Ntlemeza's application for leave to appeal was turned down by the High Court on 20 January 2016. The following day, newspaper billboards on Durban's highways and byways welcomed Booysen back:

HANDS OFF BOOYSEN ... COURT
BOOYSEN PLEASED WITH HIGH COURT DECISION
BACK TO WORK FOR FORMER HAWKS BOSS

Two days before Johan was due to return to the office, Ntlemeza announced he would be petitioning the Supreme Court of Appeal. He had taken legal advice, his spokesman Hangwani Mulaudzi said in a statement: 'Ntlemeza has decided to take the matter further by instructing his attorneys to file a petition with the Supreme Court of Appeal against the judgment of the High Court.'

When Ntlemeza was asked by journalists at a news conference to explain why he was persisting when the High Court had overturned Booysen's suspension, Minister of Police Nathi Nhleko, sitting next to him, hastily intervened: 'I have just asked General Ntlemeza not to respond to those questions precisely because what we should be able to respect around legal issues is to observe the processes that are unfolding. The issue pertaining to General Booysen is a matter before our courts ...'

'Nhleko Shields Ntlemeza from Booysen Questions,' was the headline on eNCA on 24 January.

But he couldn't shield Ntlemeza from himself, Johan thought.

He was clearly frantic about the possibility of me returning to work. He seemed to be more interested in protecting provincial commissioner Ngobeni and company than protecting the public against crime. In petitioning the Supreme Court of Appeal to overturn the ruling, he claimed that I had been party to the selection of his successor and had been interviewed for the job himself.

Ntlemeza had written: 'Another person (Zikhali) has been appointed in the position occupied by the first respondent (Booysen). This was done pursuant to a process which the first respondent (Booysen) participated in and was also interviewed but was unsuccessful.'

Johan filed a supplementary affidavit in the Supreme Court of Appeal, saying he hadn't been part of the process to elect his successor, nor had he been interviewed: 'While it is correct that another person (Zikhali) has been appointed in my position despite the fact that I continue to occupy that position, it is untrue that this person (Zikhali) was appointed pursuant to a process which I participated in.'

Ntlemeza replied that the original affidavit had been 'a draft submitted by my lawyer and signed and accidentally submitted to the court'. He admitted that Johan hadn't been part of the process.

Johan reported him to IPID for what he believed was perjury.

It wasn't the first time that he'd been accused of lying under oath and he needed to realise he couldn't carry on doing it. If not a blatant lie, it certainly demonstrated his incompetence. He, more than anyone, needed to be aware of the importance of deposing an affidavit. It was outrageous that the head of a specialised unit couldn't draft a proper document to the SCA. That's our core business: affidavits, investigations, legal documents. But he wanted to charge me for fraud for a typo that Willie Olivier made?

IPID's Robbie Raburabu confirmed that it was investigating a complaint of perjury – and Ntlemeza was in the news again for all the wrong reasons:

NEWS24
30 MARCH 2016
NTLEMEZA 'DIDN'T READ AFFIDAVIT' SUBMITTED TO SCA - REPORT

Cape Town – The saga between the national head of the police's top crime-fighting unit and its KwaZulu-Natal boss has taken yet another turn.

The Hawks' top officer Major General Berning Ntlemeza has

been accused of trying to mislead the Supreme Court of Appeal in a statement surrounding the matter against KZN Hawks boss Johan Booysen. Eyewitness News reported on Wednesday that Ntlemeza stated in an affidavit that Booysen 'was party to the process to appoint his successor' and Booysen was also interviewed for the role. But Booysen showed in a supplementary affidavit that this was untrue, the broadcaster stated.'

It was, Johan thought, becoming rather like a long-running soap opera.

Mondli Makhanya had once written an article in *City Press* called 'Crisis in the days of our lives'. TV soapies, he said, had nothing on the ongoing drama in the crumbling criminal justice system: 'It is ruthless and ugly. And debilitating. Fuelled by rumour mongering, uncertainty and extreme paranoia, the intrigue in this drama reaches right up to the highest office and deep down into the bowels of our law enforcement agencies.'

At the top, Makhanya wrote, was a president so afraid of a revived prosecution that he appointed and fired people on the basis of who could keep him out of orange prison overalls. 'And lurking somewhere in the dark and pulling invisible strings is a man who wields mysterious power: Richard Mdluli. What this power is can only be determined if someone lays their hand on the key to the safe that keeps South Africa's darkest secrets.'

Not only secrets – Johan suspected that Mdluli continued to have a hand in who benefited from the multimillion-rand police slush fund.

Johan had a deep-throat at the NPA. He had heard that tried-and-trusted former Asset Forfeiture Unit head Advocate Willie Hofmeyr, a stickler for legal compliance, had been moved sideways.

All cases dealing with unethical conduct by Jiba had been removed from Hofmeyr's files so that Shaun Abrahams could deal with them 'personally', said the source.

Word was that Jiba was hunting for the Panday docket, the one which alleged that he had asked Kevin Stephen to manufacture invoices. Johan had tried and failed to get it back on the court roll in KZN via state prosecutor Dorian Paver. At first, says Johan, the extremely articulate

Paver was eager to proceed. When he met him in Pietermaritzburg in 2015 to discuss the case, Johan says Paver agreed to get the documentation from IPID to have the case reinstated.

Then he went quiet, which puzzled Johan.

He went from ready to go to extremely reluctant. He began making excuses: first he said that Kevin Stephen was a reluctant witness, which he wasn't, then he came up with a comment that spoke volumes.

When asked if he would still be pursuing the matter, Paver said he wasn't prepared to commit 'career suicide'. Johan was disappointed.

This was a prosecutor who should have shown neither fear nor favour. Now he didn't want to get on the wrong side of Shaun Abrahams, who was protecting Jiba. It's an open secret that she played a role to get Abrahams appointed so she could call the shots.

When approached for comment, Paver said that the bottom line was that the decision to prosecute Panday wasn't his to make.

In an affidavit made in February 2016, former AFU head Willie Hofmeyr said that the new national director of Public Prosecutions had become part of a 'systematic pattern of protecting Jiba'. It was a protection pattern that stretched all the way to Number One, thought Johan. With rejuvenated confidence, Jiba proceeded to use her authority and power to settle scores; Advocate Glynnis Breytenbach and General Johan Booysen were near the top of her list it seemed.

•

Then, on 16 February 2016, two years after the NPA had withdrawn charges of racketeering against Johan, they were reinstated. NDPP Shaun Abrahams signed authority for him to be recharged. In the meantime, the Cato Manor members had applied for the charges against them, authorised by Jiba, to be set aside. Abrahams, through the state attorney, had opposed this review application.

Now, even though the Jiba authorisation to prosecute Cato Manor was still valid, Abrahams inexplicably signed another. Anticipating that the review application would be successful, he made sure the second certificates were ready and waiting.

It was clearly a mistake, Johan says.

A week later he wrote to our lawyer Carl and withdrew Jiba's authorisation. According to case law, he had no authority to do this. It has to be done via the courts. Why oppose the review application to have the authorisation set aside then withdraw it yourself later on?

Abrahams even signed authorisation to prosecute deceased Cato Manor member Neville Eva.

It was outrageous reasoning, Johan thought.

There was no sane reason for including a dead man. It could only have been because they hadn't even bothered to revise the application. But instead of admitting it was an oversight, the NPA said it was because 'reference would be made to the deceased during the trial'. It indicated to me that Shaun Abrahams was merely doing the bidding of Jiba. He had just rubber-stamped the charges and I don't think he even read them. If he had he would have noticed that the indictment and the authorisation he'd signed were at odds with each other.

Although the second indictment listed 30 accused, one of them, accused number 29, Pillay, didn't appear on either of the indictments, or the authorisation to prosecute.

Pillay had appeared in court 15 times, his name was listed as an accused, but according to the indictment he hadn't committed any offence at all. Also left off was accused number 19, Thomas Dlamuka. Abrahams signed for a dead person and left out someone who was still alive. He appeared completely out of his depth. This was the man heading the National Prosecuting Authority.

Another of the Cato Manor accused, Mukesh Panday, had committed more than one predicate offence, but wasn't charged for racketeering. One of the requirements for racketeering is that more than one predicate offence be committed within a ten-year period. Although the indictment said there were 30 accused, two of whom were dead, only 17 were charged for racketeering. Crazy, Johan thought.

Racketeering is serious – according to the Prevention of Organised Crime Act, POCA, it can get you life imprisonment and a fine of up to a million rand. Yet Abrahams treated it without the necessary gravitas. Carl van der Merwe had consulted with racketeering expert Michael Johnson in the United States, under whom I'd trained, and he said he'd never seen such a sloppy indictment.

That same day NPA spokesman Advocate Luvoyo Mfaku told Stephen

Grootes on Talk Radio 702 that Advocate Abrahams, having considered the 'strength of the evidence against General Booysen and members of the Cato Manor Organised Crime Unit' had decided that there was a prosecutable prima facie case and 'had therefore issued a certificate for them to be prosecuted on racketeering charges'.

SG: Is this a vendetta against Booysen?

NPA: There is no vendetta against Booysen. We are aware of the conspiracy theories that are aimed at discrediting the NPA for upholding the constitution. We really do not take cognisance of them. They will not deter the national director from discharging his responsibilities.

SG: You say they are conspiracy theories. It was the conduct of your own organisation, the conduct of one of your four deputy heads, Advocate Nomgcobo Jiba, that was criticised by a judge. The judges uphold the Constitution in this country. How then can you say it's a conspiracy theory?

NPA: The National Director considers all the evidence contained in the docket, nothing outside the docket and therefore other considerations they are really immaterial, it is what is contained in the docket in line with prosecutorial guidelines [*sic*].

SG: You say it's not a vendetta. The NPA also tried to prosecute the Cato Manor Organised Crime Squad as a death squad, claiming they were killing people for money, that has not been substantiated, the evidence did not stand up, now you are laying charges against them as well? It's going to look like a vendetta to anyone not involved in the case.

NPA: There is no vendetta ... we will introduce evidence in court. Just wait for the date of the trial and then follow the trial and the criminal proceedings as they unfold.

SG: Are you able to tell us then if this is new evidence that we haven't heard about before?

NPA: Let's wait for the trial to commence, let's wait for the criminal process to unfold.

Three days later, on 19 February, Johan was arrested again, shortly before appearing in the Durban High Court with the Cato Manor. He had thought they might do this to intimidate him, so went to Durban Central police station early to be fingerprinted and processed. There he found his old friend, Colonel Ncube, who in 2012 had insisted on bringing the Task Force to handcuff him in his office.

On this occasion he lost no time in popping Johan into a cell.

When Johan asked him the reason for his arrest and whether the state had new evidence against him, Colonel Ncube assured him that 'nothing had changed'. At 10am Johan emerged from the court cells and sat down next to the rest of the Cato Manor team. He had last seen them all together two months before at a pre-Christmas lunch in Camperdown. They had had a few drinks and tried not to talk about the case. Middle-aged men, once top detectives, sitting around waiting for a trial that still hadn't got off the ground after four years and 13 court appearances.

In court, Johan whispered to accused number 2, Paddy Padayachee, who had become accused number one in his absence:

Thanks for keeping my seat warm.

Just before the start of Cato Manor's fourteenth court appearance, Johan asked Carl van der Merwe to find out what new evidence the state had. They must have come up with something new if they were recharging him. Holding up the list of witnesses and the indictment, Carl asked state prosecutor Raymond Mathenjwa if anything had changed.

The witnesses, said Mathenjwa, remained the same, as did the indictment.

Nothing had changed. Aris Danikas still wasn't on the witness list. Johan had been told that a high-level delegation had gone to Greece to try to persuade Danikas to at least sign his statement. They had been unsuccessful. Johan could only shake his head in disbelief.

ROUND SEVEN

Four years had passed but they presented the same charges – the charges that the state's counsel had withdrawn against me two years previously. Like Jiba the first time around, Abrahams had not applied his mind when he signed the certificate.

For four years Johan had been upbeat and positive, and convinced that he would return to work. Now he was feeling dejected despite the court victories.

It didn't matter what the courts ruled – it seemed the NPA would just carry on and on until I was out of their way. No matter how many times I beat them in court, they would continue litigating until I disappeared off their radar. I had 16 months left before I retired. I wanted to fight criminals – but I was getting fed up with fighting the system. There had been so many of them: Mthethwa, Mduli, Ngobeni, Jiba, Mabula, Phiyega, Noko, Nhleko, Ntlemeza, the Sunday Times, *Thoshan Panday and his political connections. So many protagonists with so many agendas.*

- 21 -

BLOOD ON THEIR HANDS

In between meetings, preparing court papers and consulting with his lawyers, Johan tries to forget about it all. His daughter, Natalie, and her husband are building a house in Gauteng and he busies himself on the construction site. In the evenings, the family meets up for dinner. They joke around, but the situation weighs heavily on them. His eldest son, Morné, affectionately calls Johan '*hardegat*' (hard arse) but says he can see that the stress of the ongoing court cases is taking its toll on him.

'At his age he should be enjoying life,' Morné says. 'Instead, he's fighting for what's right and he's frustrated that he can't be doing his job as a policeman. He wants to retire as General Booysen.'

Johan, very much the patriarch, is deferred to and they put up with his occasional moods. The only ones who don't seem nervous of him are four-year-old Mila, who has inherited her grandfather's dimples, and her mother, his daughter-in-law Liza, who says:

> We call him *Donderbossie* [thundercloud] – because he has a short fuse at times – but who wouldn't with the stuff he's had to put up with? I phoned him one day and told him that even though I wasn't his flesh and blood I wanted him to know that his children were

proud of him, even if they don't tell him. He is leaving a legacy that will live on even when he is dead.

•

On the afternoon of 30 March 2016, Johan had another meeting. This time it was with Robert McBride in Durban. The suspended IPID head had recently himself appeared in court on fraud charges, at the behest, McBride thought, of Nathi Nhleko and Berning Ntlemeza, ostensibly for protecting former Hawks head Anwa Dramat.

Bemused by the ongoing efforts to nail them, Johan and McBride discussed what drove them.

Carrots or sticks drive human beings. Our livelihoods, our reputations are our carrots.

McBride laughed: 'Sometimes I want to disappear and go fishing in the sunset. But my country is my carrot.'

My stick is the public out there. They give me hope because enough people sharing the same values can bring about change.

He told Robert of how recently in Camperdown a man who had identified himself as a public prosecutor had approached him: 'I am praying for you, God is watching you. What Jiba is doing to you is wrong.'

In shopping centres and in the street, people come up to Johan and tell him not to give up. They seem to love a fighter. In church someone slips him a note: 'Brother ... may this comfort and guide you in your time of need, with God nothing is impossible. We wish you strength and our prayers are with you.'

One day in Pretoria, a young man cut Johan off in the traffic and then jumped a red light. Johan followed him until he stopped at a garage, approached the young man and told him he was driving recklessly. The advice wasn't well received.

He told me to f-off, so I said I was a cop and took him to the Silverton Police Station across the road and gave him a lecture about speaking to his elders with respect. I took down his details and we started corresponding. Now when he reads something in the news about me he fires off an email.

CMashaba@

Date: 04 April 2016 at 8:49:22 AM SAST

To: Johan Booysen

Hi major, I hope you well and I hope the case was put to rest, I don't understand why it was reinstated because there's no case, this was political motivated, even this guy ntlemeza he lied.

•

Nothing, Johan is fond of saying, with apologies to Jacques Cousteau, predicts the actions of a shark.

Normally you are able to work out how people will react. But with the current head of the Hawks and the rest of the cabal, there is no predicting their reasoning. They have so many agendas and counter-agendas the only predictable thing about them is that they are unpredictable. There can be blood in the water and they won't bite – then they savage you when you least expect it.

On the morning of the same day he'd met with McBride, a shark had come circling. This time in the form of Major General Alfred Khana, the same person who had acted in Johan's position when he was first suspended. Khana was now based at Hawks HQ in Pretoria, but he had come to Durban on what Johan assumed was a mission for Ntlemeza. Khana said he needed to see Willie Olivier too, so there were no prizes for guessing what it was about, thought Johan. Fraud seemed to be Ntlemeza's latest sjambok.

It was quite ironic because Khana himself had once been under investigation for fraud and had resigned from SAPS. He'd maintained he'd been wrongly accused. Now he was after me on trumped-up charges.

Johan met Khana at a coffee shop in Florida Road. Johan in shorts and slipslops, General Khana smart in khakis and a striped shirt, one pair of spectacles on his head, another on the end of his nose. He seemed uncomfortable, Johan thought.

With him was a brigadier. He told me they'd been sent to take warning statements from me and Willie with a view to charging us for fraud for falsely claiming for monetary awards – the same internal fraud charges that Judge Van Zyl had overturned in the decision that Ntlemeza was challenging at the SCA.

Johan asked Khana what the exact allegations were and where and when they had been committed.

I knew that if there was a case Jiba would want one of her handpicked prosecutors in Pretoria to do it. But to be heard in Pretoria, the offence needed to have been committed there. I told him that I wasn't going to be accused of committing a crime in Pretoria if I hadn't been there at the time. And if it was committed in Durban, to tell Ntlemeza that charges must be laid in Durban.

General Khana, in a corner, went to confer with the brigadier, who was trying to construct a warning statement with Olivier at a table on the pavement outside. Johan thought he also looked extremely out of sorts.

They were both skirting around the issue, not wanting to answer our questions or admit that they were pursuing someone else's agenda.

Johan told them neither he nor Olivier had signed anything in Pretoria on the date they mentioned. He was getting tired of repeating that the awards had been approved and signed by the National Awards Committee.

He felt like telling Khana to stop being a stooge. That he should have refused to come to Durban without even asking questions of those who had sent him. Instead he said to him:

I know and you know why the docket has been registered in Pretoria.

General Khana and the brigadier disappeared back to Pretoria, never to be seen again. But Johan followed up by email, asking Khana and the brigadier how the investigation was going and if they had any more details. There was no response. He sent another email:

'Is the investigation still alive? Do you still need an explanation from us – viz Olivier and Booysen? If indeed, please provide a full description of the alleged offence:

- Exactly how was it committed? A generalised allegation does not suffice.
- What is the exact nature of the misrepresentation?

- Who did we mislead?
- On exactly what dates did we commit the alleged offence – on the same or on different dates?
- Where was the offence committed?'

In the meanwhile, Johan had met with Lieutenant Generals Hamilton Ngidi, André Pruis and Magda Stander, who had either signed the monetary awards, or been on the Awards Committee. They had agreed to attest to approving the awards. Johan asked in his email why Khana or the brigadier hadn't spoken to them as part of the investigation:

> 'We are indeed perplexed and place on record that you have not approached these witnesses before approaching us for warning statements. It shows ... bias in your investigation since these witnesses' statements indicate ... that no misrepresentation was made.
>
> We have previously requested (6th instance) to proceed in obtaining their statements ourselves. You have not responded. We hereby repeat that request.
>
> Lastly – we have taken note of the judgment in a fraud case ... against Major General Shadrack Sibiya. In that case the prosecutor made a startling statement to the magistrate after Sibiya's acquittal ...'

Former Gauteng Hawks head, Sibiya, who had investigated Richard Mdluli, was acquitted of fraud in April 2016. He'd been charged for using his private car for work, for which he had claimed around R24 000. His PA, who had filled in the form, had claimed for Sibiya's new car, instead of his old one. Although it had resulted in him under-claiming, Ntlemeza and the Hawks had waded in and charged him anyway. The case fell short in court.

When questioned, the state prosecutor told the magistrate that he had been 'instructed by his seniors to proceed with the prosecution' even though there wasn't a case. The NPA denied this was said in court, although the prosecutor is on record:

> Your Worship ... I should also add ... that when the matter was placed on the roll, I did place on record and I will place it again

your Worship, that this matter was a result of the background given by the IO, but more so ... it was because of the instruction that came from the office that the accused should be charged. Therefore the state will concede, your Worship, that not all four elements of fraud are proven by the state ...

Not long after that email to Khana, Johan would see Sibiya himself. Late in April, Johan was invited to a meeting at the Nelson Mandela Foundation HQ in Johannesburg. Details were sketchy and he wasn't sure what to expect. As he parked his car, he saw Robert McBride. Inside the venue were Shadrack Sibiya and one of Anwa Dramat's brothers. There was also a contingent of ex-SARS employees – Ivan Pillay, Johan van Loggerenberg, Adrian Lackay and Yolisa Pikie. The SARS contingent had also, in Johan's opinion, been a victim of the *Sunday Times* and Crime Intelligence. Stephan Hofstatter, Mzilikazi Wa Afrika and Piet Rampedi had, in October 2014, reported that Pillay and Van Loggerenberg, with the knowledge of Finance Minister Pravin Gordhan, ran a rogue unit, operated a brothel and spied on Jacob Zuma.

The press ombudsman had ordered the *Sunday Times* to apologise and to retract its SARS rogue unit stories. The newspaper's new editor, Bongani Siqoko, admitted that under its previous editor, Phylicia Oppelt, it had 'got some things wrong' and:

> In particular ... [the newspaper had] stated some allegations as fact, and gave incomplete information in some cases ... In trying to inform you about SARS, we should have provided you with all the dimensions of the story and not overly relied on our sources ... The SARS story has given us an opportunity to take a closer look at our news-gathering and production processes. We have found some serious gaps.
>
> Efforts are being made to close those. Our news desk – made up of a team of section editors – is being restructured.

Johan had also reported the *Sunday Times* to the press ombudsman for getting 'some things wrong' and for 'overly relying on sources'. In

February 2016, he had sat across a table from journalists Stephan Hofstatter and Mzilikazi Wa Afrika, but because the NPA had just recharged him, the hearing was postponed.

Now gathered in the same room at the Mandela Foundation was a bunch of once high-ranking state officials who all had a common experience with a government institution. Their subsequent removal had followed a pattern, they thought, emanating from an 'engine room' comprising people such as Minister Nathi Nhleko, Nomgcobo Jiba, Richard Mdluli and others with the president's interests at heart. Invariably, documents had been leaked to selected journalists, always working with anonymous sources. There would be an 'exposé' in the paper, then an 'investigation' into the accused officials, often using the false news reports as the pretext. During the 'investigations' the affected officials were suspended to neutralise them and they were seldom called to answer allegations. They were expected to carry the cost of their own legal defence although the trumped-up charges were supposedly committed in the workplace. Those pursuing the agenda relied on unlimited state resources – taxpayers' money.

A month later, at a second meeting of the newly formed group, this time at a hotel in Pretoria, Robert McBride's fellow accused Matthew Sesoko and Innocent Khuba joined them. Khuba, from IPID in Limpopo, had investigated the illegal rendition of the Zimbabwean suspects, for which Shadrack Sibiya and Anwa Dramat had been suspended.

Khuba said he had been told to collaborate with Crime Intelligence during the investigation, but not to tell anyone, which he had found odd. His worst fears about the arrangement were confirmed, he wrote in an affidavit, when information from the docket implicating Dramat began appearing in the *Sunday Times*. It got worse when Berning Ntlemeza, then deputy police commissioner in Limpopo, whom he knew well, asked to meet with him. He brought with him a witness whom he said could assist in the rendition case. Khuba had grave doubts about the veracity of the witness's statement. But Ntlemeza kept up the pressure, phoning him on Khuba's wife's phone – and arriving at his house to tell him that he shouldn't be afraid because Richard Mdluli was looking out for him. Khuba wrote:

He said he was asked by Mdluli to deploy people for my safety and
that if I see any suspicious car behind me I should call him ... I
was surprised because I never met or spoke with Mdluli ... What
General Ntlemeza said to me got me worried. I spoke to my wife
saying that by accepting the request to investigate the rendition
case, I do not know what I got myself in to ...

The next time Khuba saw Ntlemeza was in December 2014 when Ntlemeza told him his 'time to move to the Hawks had arrived'. Soon afterwards, Ntlemeza was appointed acting Hawks head.

Khuba's affidavit continued:

The Hawks members have been to my house four times now
regarding the same case. I shiver to the core of my spine with fear
because I realise I investigated a case so politically charged to an
extent that certain outcomes were needed. I was fired without a
hearing and that seems to have not been enough. These charges
of defeating the ends of justice and fraud are as baffling as my
departmental case itself ... I fear for my personal safety because
members of the Hawks have already made advances, asking me to
make a statement that implicates McBride and Seseko in order to
be reinstated to my position.

Now under the auspices of a Public Administration Research Institute exploring the 'dynamics affecting performance of government departments and agencies', Khuba, the other IPID officials and the ex-SARS group had been brought together to help highlight the abuse of state resources and the capture of democratic institutions. Johan was with them. He wasn't going to give in to what he regarded as a cabal driven by fear.

Nobody will pursue individuals so relentlessly without being motivated by fear: fear of prosecution, fear of being found out, fear of falling out of favour. I don't have that fear because I'm not guilty of anything. If I were, I would've given up long ago. I wouldn't be taking on the minister, the head of the DPCI, the NPA and the provincial commissioner. My crusade relates to unlawful and ongoing persecution and abuse of scarce state resources.

•

Out of the blue, at a shop in Durban North, Johan bumps into Thoshan Panday.

Panday gives him a thumbs-up. 'Strong?' he asks.

Very, says Johan, returning the thumbs up, but feeling like knocking him off his feet.

•

On April Fools Day in 2016 Johan and Cato Manor returned to court. The case was postponed again, for the fifteenth time, for Cato Manor, to January 2017. By that time, Johan thought, he would have been a policeman for 40 years. He didn't want to enter 2017 and his retirement year with a court case hanging over him. He decided to mount another challenge.

Jiba's original decision to prosecute us for racketeering was unjustified and unconstitutional. I planned to ask the Court to review Abrahams' latest decision to authorise prosecution against me.

He flew to Cape Town to meet Advocate Anton Katz and his team, and they discussed their strategy. Katz had been Johan's advocate in the Gorven judgment against Jiba. Now, they contended, by reinstating those charges, Jiba's replacement, Abrahams, was attempting to undermine the legitimacy and finality of that judgment. The national director of public prosecutions was, they believed, guilty of contempt of court.

In early June, Abrahams provided the record that he considered as new evidence. It included a memorandum from state prosecutor Sello Maema and a PowerPoint presentation by KZN prosecutions head Moipone Noko. Johan says both documents contained untruths.

In the presentation, Noko said Aris Danikas was a witness, which he never was. She also outrageously stated that he was my son-in-law. How Abrahams accepted this to reinstate charges against me is inconceivable.

And in Maema's prosecution memo to Abrahams, he says that Cato Manor had no evidence against any of the suspects they shot and that there were no warrants for their arrests. But there were five warrants for arrest and, in any event, in terms of the Criminal Procedure Act an officer of the law doesn't need a warrant, he or she needs 'reasonable grounds' to suspect that the suspect has committed a first-schedule offence.

Johan laid charges of fraud and defeating the ends of justice against Maema at Silverton Police Station in Pretoria. His statement read:

'Of the 28 people shot over a period of four years there was direct evidence linking 25 of them – such as eye witnesses, statements of co-accused, fingerprints, CCTV footage, cellphone mapping, cellphone records.'

On Sunday 19 June, Johan drove to Pietermaritzburg, where Noko's offices were, and also laid charges against her for fraud and defeating the ends of justice. He had it on reliable authority that she had a phalanx of bodyguards outside her house in Durban, even an armoured vehicle. He suspected she enjoyed the aura of being KZN's top prosecutor. But nothing could protect her from the law, he reasoned.

In her PowerPoint presentation, Noko said there was no evidence linking Bongani Mkhize to Inkosi Zondi's murder. But there was – the written confession from Swayo Mkhize that he, Bongani, as well as Sifiso and Badumile Ndimande had plotted the murders at Steers in Durban North. Noko also repeated the lie that Willie Olivier and I had tampered with the Howick scene by placing an AK-47 near where Magojela Ndimande was shot. Where is the evidence, I ask again? Over and above the lies I believed Maema and Noko had presented to Abrahams, there were a number of misrepresentations of facts contained in the dockets, as well as omissions. Ten of the deceased had tested positive for primer residue on their hands, indicating that they had fired guns. You can't just exclude it. They had also omitted to mention that firearms found on some of the deceased were linked by ballistics to cartridges found at the scenes.

Curiously, in the record sent to Johan by Abrahams, a statement appeared that he had never seen before. It was from a man called Simphiwe Mathonsi, of whom Johan had never heard. The statement was dated 15 June 2013. In it, Mathonsi, a taxi security guard, claimed to have overheard a discussion about a plot to kill Lieutenant Colonel Chonco. He stated: 'I heard them saying Chonco was a trouble and they will talk to senior officer [sic] referring to Booysen and Mostert to sort him out [Chonco].'

But in his memorandum to Abrahams, Maema appears to twist what Mathonsi says, so it comes across that it was Johan and Mossie Mostert who had conspired to kill Chonco: 'This witness heard Mostert and Booysen planning to kill Chonco. But they did not want to do it themselves, they hired a hit man ...'

Maema then listed as state witnesses Mathonsi, along with Aiyer and Ndlondlo, although they weren't on the list presented in court by his colleague, Raymond Mathenjwa, on 19 February. Maema stated: 'The following witnesses will testify about the role of Booysen in the management of the SVC Section based at Cato Manor and that he had more close links section more [sic] than any other section in the Organised Crime.'

Johan made inquiries and found out that Mathonsi had died of natural causes in 2014.

Conveniently, Mathonsi was dead so he couldn't present this evidence in court. But dead or alive, Maema was misrepresenting evidence. He and his investigators hadn't bothered to even speak to the person Mathonsi had allegedly overheard. I was sick of it – Maema had also lied to say that Ndlondlo had been killed. So I laid charges of perjury against him for that too.

In late June 2016, Johan met with former NPA head Mxolisi Nxasana in Durban. Nxasana told him that while he was still in office, Jiba and Maema had relentlessly badgered him to reauthorise Johan's prosecution. Nxasana described them as having virtually 'camped outside his door'. He said he'd told them repeatedly that unless there was compelling new evidence he couldn't do so. No sooner had Nxasana been removed than Noko and Maema approached his successor, Abrahams, with so-called 'new' detail.

What was contained in their presentations did not coincide with what was in the dockets. If Abrahams had read the dockets, with the same lack of evidence, untruths and misrepresentations, alarm bells should have rung. I could only shake my head when I heard him on national TV saying he wasn't a political lackey.

•

By the end of June 2016, Johan had laid criminal charges against Ntlemeza, Noko and Maema, challenged the investigators and prosecutors seven times, winning six applications with costs. The seventh, the review of the fresh racketeering charges, was pending. He had made a statement to the Bar Council to have Jiba struck off the roll as an advocate and lodged a civil claim against the minister of police, as well as Hawks investigators Jan Mabula and Pharasa Ncube, Jiba and Glen Angus of IPID. He also intended suing Abrahams, Jiba and Maema for malicious prosecution.

He was determined not to allow people within the criminal justice system he was once part of to get away with blood on their hands.

Criminals carry on terrorising the public, while the system shuts down an effective crime-fighting unit like Cato Manor and then pursues an insidious agenda against me. I was born to be a policeman and I want to be remembered for being a good policeman. If the last thing I do is to expose those destroying the criminal justice system, I'll be happy. I'm not the only one who thinks that Jiba and her cabal have blood on their hands. It's now widely acknowledged that they are protecting themselves and their cohorts from prosecution.

Complacency will allow people like her and Richard Mdluli to capture vital state institutions to advance their own financial and other interests. That's why I won't back off. Many people turn silent when faced by injustice, but it's apathy that creates a breeding ground for the evil monsters that will in the end devour us all.

Speak up when you see that something is wrong – don't be silent, even if you should suffer anguish. Democracy is a living creature – if we are paralysed by fear, it will become extinct.

Get involved, write to your local paper, phone your local authority; make public officials accountable – they are there to render a service. It's your country and it's your right. The Irish statesman Edward Burke once said: for evil to triumph, good men must do nothing. That's my motto.

POSTSCRIPT

As this book went to reprint in September 2016, there had been several significant developments.

On 2 September, National Director of Public Prosecutions Shaun Abrahams announced that the National Prosecuting Authority would prosecute Thoshan Panday and Colonel Navin Madhoe for 'attempting to bribe Hawks boss Johan Booysen'.

Johan found the timing suspicious. Not long before, he had applied for a review of Abrahams' decision to authorise his prosecution. He had also lodged an official complaint with the General Council of the Bar to investigate the conduct of Advocates Moipone Noko and Sello Maema whom, he said, had lied and misrepresented the case against him. Their prosecution memoranda, on which Abrahams had apparently relied, contained, in Johan's opinion, 'more fiction than fact, more speculation than evidence and misled far more than it informed'.

Abrahams, Johan said in an affidavit, had either been complicit in the deception, or negligent.

I saw his sudden turnaround regarding Panday as a cynical and strategic move. Gerrie Nel's recommendations had been lying on his desk for 18 months. Now, because I'd accused Abrahams in court papers of indirectly protecting Panday, he was obliged to respond. What about the two other cases against Panday? The evidence is clear.

On 6 September, the Constitutional Court ruled that Police Minister Nathi Nhleko's decision to suspend IPID head Robert McBride was unlawful.

Then, on 15 September, Abrahams' deputy at the NPA, Nomgcobo Jiba, and the NPA's Commercial Crimes head, Lawrence Mrwebi, were struck from the roll of advocates. The Pretoria High Court had been asked to rule on their handling of three 'highly political' cases: the decisions to drop charges against Jacob Zuma and Richard Mdluli and their 'insistence on prosecuting KZN Hawks' head, Johan Booysen'.

Judge Frans Legodi with Judge W Hughes said Jiba had 'flouted every rule in the fight against crime'. Her failure to intervene when required to do so had 'failed the citizens of this country and in the process, brought the image of the legal profession and prosecuting authority into disrepute. Both Mrwebi and Jiba should be found to have ceased to be fit and proper persons to remain on a roll of advocates.'

Jiba and Mrwebi have indicated their intention to appeal the rulings.

I stand by what I have said. These public officials have abused the power vested in them. They should not be permitted to force the taxpayer to incur the costs of their unlawful actions.

NOTES

1. Bill Freund. December 2013. 'Social Order and Organisation in Vanderbijlpark and Sasolburg: The Company Towns of the Vaal Triangle 1940–90'. Paper delivered at the 8th New Frontiers in African Economic History Workshop, Lund.

2. Sarah M Mathis. 'From War Leaders to Freedom Fighters: Forms of Violence in Umbumbulu in the 1980s and 90s'. *Journal of Natal and Zulu History*. KZN HAAS. 27 April 2005. Accessed 25 June 2016. http://www.kznhass-history.net/files/seminars/Mathis2005.pdf. Unpublished paper. Permission from author.

3. *TRC Final Report.* 15 April 2016. Accessed 25 June 2016. http://sabctrc.saha.org.za/reports/volume3/chapter3/subsection31.htm. Volume 3, Chapter 3, Sub-Section 31.

4. Mathis, 'From War Leaders to Freedom Fighters'.

5. Vusi Pikoli and Mandy Wiener. 2014. *My Second Initiation: The Memoir of Vusi Pikoli*. Pan Macmillan South Africa, page 353.

ACKNOWLEDGEMENTS

To Nicky, whose idea it was; to Brenda, Joy, Phillippa, Mary and William for lodgings and writing havens in Nottingham Road, Hilton, Pietermaritzburg and Durban; to Andrea N and all at Pan Macmillan for infinite patience and professionalism; and to my late uncle Theo for the means to make it happen.

Jessica Pitchford
Johannesburg, July 2016

•

To protect and serve

I have lived my passion. My 40-year career with the police has been extraordinary. I have worked with some amazingly talented police officers and I salute each one of them. Thank you to those who stood by me while I faced persecution: my church, my colleagues and the public who urged me to seek justice.

To my family, whose unwavering support helped me through challenging times, I know the pain and uncertainty you have suffered.

In the dark corridors of power, truth is often the first casualty of those who will stop at nothing to achieve their goals, allowing graft and deceit to triumph and riding roughshod over whomever stands in their way.

ACKNOWLEDGEMENTS

Understanding the dynamics behind why my colleagues and I were persecuted, why the National Prosecuting Authority targeted me, why some within the Directorate of Priority Crime Investigation and the cabinet wanted me gone, is complex. There isn't a simple answer, but there is a fairly simple recipe. It takes several protagonists, each with an agenda and a common enemy; a handful of useful idiots and a shoal of circling sharks.

Such a recipe has the ability to create a perfect storm, similar to the one that hit me in 2011. It has left many casualties in its five-year wake.

This is my story. This is my truth.

Johan W Booysen
Durban, July 2016